The World War I Memoirs
of Robert P. Patterson

The World War I Memoirs of Robert P. Patterson

A Captain in the Great War

Edited by J. Garry Clifford

LEGACIES OF WAR
G. Kurt Piehler, Series Editor

The University of Tennessee Press • Knoxville

The Legacies of War series presents a variety of works—from scholarly monographs to memoirs—that examine the impact of war on society, both in the United States and globally. The wide scope of the series might include war's effects on civilian populations, its lingering consequences for veterans, and the role of individual nations and the international community in confronting genocide and other injustices born of war.

Copyright © 2012 by The University of Tennessee Press / Knoxville.
All Rights Reserved. Manufactured in the United States of America.
Cloth: 1st printing, 2012.
Paper: 1st printing, 2018.

Library of Congress Cataloging-in-Publication Data

Patterson, Robert Porter, 1891–1952.
The World War I memoirs of Robert P. Patterson: a captain in the Great War / edited by J. Garry Clifford. — 1st ed.
    p. cm. — (Legacies of war)
Includes bibliographical references and index.
ISBN: 978-1-57233-847-0 (hardcover)
ISBN: 978-1-62190-468-7 (paperback)
1. Patterson, Robert Porter, 1891–1952.
2. World War, 1914–1918—Personal narratives, American.
3. United States. Army. Infantry Division, 77th.
4. World War, 1914–1918—Campaigns—France.
5. United States. Army. American Expeditionary Forces—Biography.
6. Soldiers—United States—Biography.
I. Clifford, J. Garry (John Garry), 1942–
II. Title.

D570.9.P37 2012
940.4'1273092—dc23
[B]
2011041683

For Robert H. Ferrell
Whose father was also a doughboy

Contents

Preface	xi
Introduction	xiii
The World War I Memoirs of Robert P. Patterson	1
Plattsburg	5
Camp Upton	11
The Ocean and England	17
With the British in Flanders	21
The Baccarat Sector	29
The Vesle Sector	35
The Aisne	51
The Argonne	55
After the Armistice	75
Infantry Equipment and Tactics	81
Appendix: Official Citations for Robert Patterson and His Men for Receiving the Distinguished Service Cross for Heroism in 1918	87
Notes	91
Bibliography	105
Index	109

Figures

Robert Patterson in World War I Uniform, 1919	xiii
Major Robert P. Patterson of the 306th Infantry Regiment, 77th Division, with Regimental Chaplain and Lieutenant, France, 1919	xvii
Robert Patterson in World War I Uniform	xviii
Private Robert Patterson of the Seventh Infantry, New York National Guard, at Camp in McAllen, Texas, July 1916	6
Panorama of the Seventh Infantry, New York National Guard, McAllen, Texas, July 4, 1916	7
Lieutenant Robert P. Patterson at Plattsburg Officers Training Camp, August 1917	8
Questionnaire Filled Out by Robert Patterson in February 1918 for Promotion to Captain	12
A Convoy at Sea	18
French 77-mm Field Gun	26
Robert Patterson with Lt. Charles DeWolf Gibson of Company K, 306th Infantry, at Triage Hospital Station in La Chalade, France, 1918	46
Saint Thibaut Church	47
Major Charles W. Whittlesey	48
Services Held in a Shell-torn Church	53
Spirit of the Argonne	57
General Robert Alexander, Who Commanded the 77th Division during the Battles of 1918	59
Major General Robert Alexander in the Office Dugout in the Argonne Forest	60
General Alexander's Dugout Headquarters from the Outside	61
Cher Ami, the Carrier Pigeon Released by Major Whittlesey, with a Message That Saved the Lost Battalion	63
The "Pocket" Where 500 Men from the 308th Regiment, 77th Division, Fought off German Forces in 1918	64

On October 8, 1918, 194 Men of the Lost Battalion Were Able to Walk out of the Pocket	69
Varennes, as Seen by a Military Artist	70
One of the Craters on the Road to Varennes, as Seen by a Military Artist	72
General John J. Pershing	79
Soldier with Browning Automatic Rifle	81
155-mm Heavy Gun	83

Maps

1. Patterson's Sketch of Trenches in British Sector, July 1918 — 23
2. The 77th Division Movements in Baccarat Sector, July 1918 — 33
3. Disposition of Forces near Bazoches, France, August 13–14, 1918 — 37
4. Patterson's Map of Firefight with Germans West of Bazoches, August 14, 1918 — 41
5. The 77th Division Movements in Vesle-Aisne Sector, August 11–September 18, 1918 — 52
6. The 77th Division in First Phase of Meuse-Argonne Offensive, September 28–October 18, 1919 — 56
7. The 77th Division in Final Meuse-Argonne Offensive, October 31–November 6, 1918 — 62
8. German Divisions Opposing 77th Division, A E.F. Argonne-Meuse Drive, 1918 — 71
9. The Final Days—November 6–11, 1918 — 73

Preface

My scholarly interest in Robert P. Patterson dates back to the early 1970s when I first met his future biographer, Keith Eiler, in the Manuscript Division at the Library of Congress. I was finishing my first book about the Plattsburg military training camp movement of 1913–20, and Keith, a retired army officer and Korean War veteran, was completing his Harvard Ph.D. dissertation on Robert Patterson's multiple contributions to victory in World War II. Because Patterson had won his commission as a "Ninety Day Wonder" at the Plattsburg Officers Training Camp in 1917, Eiler and I often talked about the values and lessons that Patterson, Henry L. Stimson, John J. McCloy, and other Plattsburg veterans of the first "Great War" brought to the second global conflict. I vividly recall one occasion when Colonel Eiler invited me to lunch at the Army-Navy Club with the cantankerous General Albert C. Wedemeyer, under whom he had served as an aide after World War II. We kept in touch over the years, sending Christmas letters and occasionally meeting at academic conferences, and when Keith's excellent study of Patterson's contributions to victory in World War II was finally published by Cornell University Press, I wrote a favorable blurb for the dust jacket. I recall my curiosity being aroused by Eiler's references to an unpublished World War I memoir by Patterson that was not in the Patterson papers at the Library of Congress.

In the spring of 2009, Robert Patterson's youngest daughter, Virginia Patterson Montgomery, contacted me about another unpublished manuscript by her father that had turned up in the files of his New York City law office. Probably written in 1948, this detailed study recounted Patterson's herculean efforts to mobilize and supply America's armed forces in World War II, and it had gathered dust for more than sixty years. Did I think such a first-person narrative should be published? After reading it, I responded affirmatively because it offered a fresh view of those wartime struggles along the Potomac by one of the key participants. Indeed, my UConn colleague, Brian Waddell, who had recently published two books about World War II mobilization issues, would be the perfect editor. When we visited Mrs. Montgomery at her colonial-era home in Stonington, Connecticut, she also surprised us by showing a photocopy of her father's World War I reminiscences, written in 1933. I read several pages, especially the section on Patterson's nearly fatal "adventure" along the Vesle River in August 1918. I was hooked. Perhaps we could find a publisher for both manuscripts. Family and friends (and biographer Eiler) had read the first memoir, and "Judge" Patterson's contemporaries understood very well how formative his World War I experiences were for his subsequent career. These reminiscences graphically re-created the "Great War" as Patterson lived it—the battles, boredom, terror, hunger, deaths, wounds, humor, friendships, exhaustion, stupidity, exhilaration, lessons, rumors, and regrets. When I made a copy and sent it to my former mentor Robert H. Ferrell, he replied that Patterson's memoir ranked among the best of the hundreds he had read in authoring his own several books on the First World War.

In preparing Patterson's manuscript for publication, I made a few minor changes in punctuation and grammar, added first names to individuals when I could check them against existing rosters, and clarified the spelling of a handful of French place-names. I am especially thankful to G. Kurt Piehler and Scot Danforth of the University of Tennessee Press for their early encouragement and faith in this project. Thanks too to Walt Evans and Stan Ivester for their careful editing. I also thank Virginia Montgomery, Robert P. Patterson Jr., and the rest of the Patterson family for numerous favors and reminiscences. Alex Reger performed technical magic in turning a "PDF" file into a "Word" file so that I could edit more effectively in a word-processing program. My friends Ted Wilson of the University of Kansas, John Chambers of Rutgers University, and Mark Stoler of the University of Vermont offered sound advice when needed. Michael Schwartz and Alejandro Corbacho graciously critiqued portions of the manuscript. I am beholden to Jennifer Keene and Edward Lengel for their incisive comments and valuable suggestions as outside readers for the University of Tennessee Press. The Patterson family ransacked their attics for vintage photos. Robert Ferrell generously made available Signal Corps photographs and maps from his own research on World War I battles. Among my colleagues at the University of Connecticut, I am always buoyed by encouragement and friendship from Mark Boyer, Larry Bowman, Frank Costigliola, Sherry Zane, Brian Waddell, Rich Hiskes, Jennifer Sterling-Folker, Christine Luberto, Jennifer Fontanella, Betty Hanson, Jeremy Pressman, and Stephen Dyson. Irv Gellman's benevolent prodding by telephone is always welcome. Of course, without my wife Carol Davidge's loving collaboration in all things, I would accomplish very little. Finally, I dedicate this book to Bob Ferrell, my friend and teacher for nearly fifty years, who wisely told me it was time to look again at the Great War.

Introduction

A journalist once called Under Secretary of War Robert P. Patterson "the toughest man in Washington" for his "all-out" efforts in managing U.S. mobilization in World War II.[1] An informal poll conducted after the war ranked Patterson second only to Army Chief of Staff General George C. Marshall as the person most responsible for America's victory over the Axis powers. The memoir that follows recounts Patterson's own formative military experiences in the First World War. Writing for his family in 1933, fifteen years after the "War to End All Wars," Patterson did not intend for his reminiscences to be published. Because he had "kept no diary" and "had no papers before me to refresh my memory," he modestly judged his "story" to be of

Robert Patterson in World War I uniform, 1919. From collection of the Patterson family.

"little interest" to the "general reader" and thus restricted it "to the events in which I took a personal part."² Nonetheless, the very personal memoir published herein is a remarkable rendering of what it was like to be a line officer of infantry during the so-called Great War.³ It tells us much about the personal experience of war and of the man himself.

Born in Glens Falls, New York, in 1891, Robert Porter Patterson graduated from Union College and Harvard Law School, and joined the distinguished Wall Street firm of Root, Clark, Buckner & Howland in 1915. Following service on the Mexican border in 1916 as a private in the New York National Guard and with America's entry into World War I, the young lawyer earned a commission as a "Ninety Day Wonder" at the first Plattsburg Officers Training Camp of 1917. As a captain in the 306th Infantry regiment of New York's famous 77th "Statue of Liberty" division, Patterson participated in the major battles from July to November 1918. In what he describes as the "greatest adventure of my life," he earned the Distinguished Service Cross for heroism during an August skirmish along the Vesle River near the tiny French village of Bazoches. Patterson's resulting bond with the citizen-soldiers of F Company endured for decades, as he kept in close touch and left legacies to several comrades when he died in January 1952. His steely determination to do all that was possible for the American "GI" in World War II stemmed from his own personal experiences in the Great War. So impressed was Patterson with the resilience and gallantry of his own doughboys that he vowed, as his biographer notes, that "no effort should be spared in reciprocating their trust and promoting their welfare."⁴ "We do not ask our boys in combat to do an adequate job," he would say. "We ask them to do their best. We can do no less."⁵

President Herbert Hoover appointed Patterson in 1930 as the U.S. District Court judge of the Southern District of New York, and in 1939 President Franklin D. Roosevelt elevated him to the U.S. Circuit Court of Appeals for the Second Circuit. Despite such exalted standing as a jurist, the forty-nine-year-old Patterson was obediently performing Kitchen Police (KP) duty at another Plattsburg training camp in July 1940 when he was promoted from "private" to become assistant secretary of war.⁶ Despite his personal preference for active service as a combat infantry officer, Patterson heeded the call to become Secretary Henry L. Stimson's principal collaborator in running the War Department for the next five years.⁷ As assistant secretary and then under secretary of war, Patterson negotiated the contracts and supervised the delivery of more than a hundred billion dollars' worth of supplies and equipment to America's far-flung forces in World War II. President Harry S. Truman nearly appointed Patterson to the U.S.

Supreme Court before naming him to succeed Stimson as secretary of war in September 1945. The new secretary led the fight for unification of the armed forces under the National Security Act of 1947 and the creation of the Defense Department. His appointment of and strong support for the Gillem Board's recommendations in 1946 for the postwar utilization of "Negro Manpower" laid the foundation for President Truman's executive order to desegregate the armed forces two years later.[8] Patterson returned to his law practice in 1947 and later served as president of the Council on Foreign Relations and president of the Association of the Bar of the City of New York prior to his untimely death in a plane crash at age sixty. "He was the perfect citizen," General Marshall eulogized, "honest, courageous, self-sacrificing, and utterly sincere."[9] His remains are buried in Arlington National Cemetery.

Patterson's evocative memoir of his World War I service in the American Expeditionary Forces (AEF) deserves close reading for two important reasons. First, he recounts in understated yet vivid prose just how raw and unprepared American soldiers were for the titanic battles on the western front in 1918. Without complaint, he tells how the officers and men of Company F, 306th Regiment, Seventy-seventh Division, after minimal training in quiet British and French sectors, were thrown into combat against veteran German forces in the last months of the war. Patterson ironically downplays his own "exceedingly careless" near-death experience along the Vesle River in mid-August when he stumbled into an early morning firefight with Germans he mistakenly assumed had withdrawn—an essentially botched action for which he and several of his men nonetheless deservedly were awarded the Distinguished Service Cross. His pen portraits of fellow soldiers remain indelible. Foremost is that of his closest friend, Lieutenant Mike Hayes, "the highest type of soldier, gentleman, and American," hit in the head by a machine gun bullet as he ran down a hill near St. Juvin, literally dying in Patterson's arms. Also memorable were Sergeant Charles Johnson, the New York City fireman killed by a German artillery shell while fording the Aire River; Corporal John Miller, who stoically awaited medical treatment with his eyeball hanging down his cheek; Corporal Thomas Murphy, who lost a leg to gangrene because he could not be evacuated to the rear quickly enough; and Private Edwin "Big Ed" Duffy, shot in the jaw during the fighting for Bazoches and thought to have died in a German prison hospital, only to reappear miraculously when the 306th Infantry paraded in New York on its return from France in 1919. Patterson's reportage of the first days of the Meuse-Argonne battle rivals that of any memoirist—

the drenching cold rains, omnipresent barbed wire, deep fog-filled ravines, sweet stench of mustard gas, interminable traffic jams on narrow and twisty roads, chattering German machine guns, crashing artillery shells, green replacements who must be taught to dig funk holes, groping movement in the dark through thick underbrush to fill a mile-long gap in the line, even a rare hot meal to be savored. Like the AEF as a whole, Patterson and his company persevered by trial and error, for example, by learning to assault machine gun nests by the flank instead of frontally and eventually to coordinate rolling artillery barrages just ahead of advancing infantry. Despite his laconic comment that "the number of men killed in F Company was the smallest of any rifle company in our regiment," Patterson does not tell the reader that 26,277 doughboys died in the Meuse-Argonne offensive and 95,786 were wounded, the single deadliest battle in American history.[10] As the editor of the *Field Artillery Journal* later put it, "we muddled, but we muddled through, which was as much as anyone had a right to hope for."[11]

Perhaps even more revealing than his stark sketches of combat is the essentially positive attitude Patterson sustains throughout his reminiscences. Although writing in 1933, the former AEF captain betrays little of the postwar disillusionment that afflicted some members of the "Lost Generation." Unlike his fellow officer and historian of the 307th Infantry Regiment who in 1927 could refer to the Great War as "not altogether either crime or blunder," Patterson still saw the fighting in France as a just war and attributed the highest motives to those who served.[12] He would have rejected editor William Allen White's sardonic claim that "war is the devil's joke on humanity. So let's celebrate Armistice Day by laughing our heads off."[13]

In fact, the Patterson memoir is a paean to what one scholar has called "the national idea carried into practice."[14] Often dubbed "the melting pot division," the polyglot rank and file of New York's 77th Division consisted of immigrants and ethnic groups who spoke forty-two different languages and proudly sang their marching song: "The Jews and the Wops, / And the Dutch and the Irish cops; / they're all in the Army now."[15] As a graduate of the Plattsburg Officers Training Camp and close friend of Plattsburg leaders such as Julius Adler and Archibald Thacher, Patterson believed strongly in the democratizing benefits of universal military training. Such officers as Colonel George Vidmer of the 306th Infantry sought to "replace the barriers of class and ethnicity with a leveling standard of professionalism and common opportunity."[16] To these military progressives, it was gospel to quote Theodore Roosevelt's maxim that "the military tent, where all sleep side-by-side, will rank next to the public school among the great agents of democratization."[17] Selective service and universal military training would "Yank the hyphen out of America," Plattsburgers liked to say.[18] For Patterson, his wartime association with doughboys named Czak, Wogatzke, Lo Bono, Breitwieser, Lehmkuhl, and Finucane confirmed his faith in the democratic bonding derived from shared military obligations.[19] Just as he would write in 1922 that Jacob Drabkin and Samuel Silverstein were among "the finest fighting soldiers I have ever seen," he acknowledges in his memoir that "the conduct of Lt. Hayes and the party of five Irishmen" who tried to rescue him on the Vesle "was the bravest piece of work that came within my experience."[20] Patterson also relished reporting an incident when, out of uniform, he was watching a YMCA show just before the armistice and a soldier shoved him from behind and berated him for leaning heavily against his

Major Robert P. Paterson, center, of the 306th Infantry Regiment, 77th Division, France, 1919. Left to right, Father Thomas J. Dunne, the regimental chaplain who also earned the Distinguished Service Cross, Patterson, and an unidentified lieutenant. From collection of the Patterson family.

Robert Patterson in World War I uniform. From collection of the Patterson family.

tent. Without his captain's insignia, Patterson simply moved away and said nothing, only to learn happily after the war that one of his men had played a prank on him.

In short, World War I represented, in a sense, "the good war" for Robert P. Patterson. Despite losing friends and enduring some of the insanities of combat, the captain of infantry had survived, matured, and readied himself "for the burdens of leadership which would later fall on his shoulders" in another world war.[21] Between the wars, as he rose in the legal world as an attorney and judge, he kept up his military associations and friendships. Patterson particularly remained close to the men of Company F. As biographer Keith Eiler has written, throughout the difficult years of the Great Depression, the former doughboys of Company F continued to look to their captain as "their hero, model, and protector." His men "in an almost unheard of gesture" pooled their meager funds and presented Patterson with "an engraved silver cup, three and a half feet high." And in return, whenever any of his men ran into difficulty, "their Captain was prepared to drop everything and rush unquestioningly to his relief."[22] This unwavering commitment to service became Patterson's hallmark as he assumed the myriad duties of assistant secretary, under secretary, and then secretary of war from 1940 to 1947.

In a recent book entitled *On the Battlefield of Memory*, the literary scholar Steven Trout has argued cogently that "from the beginning," American memories of World War I have been "fractured and unsettled, more a matter of competing versions of memory—each with its own spokespeople—rather than a single, culturally pervasive reconstruction of the past."[23] Just as the novels of Ernest Hemingway and John Dos Passos painted different pictures of combat than what appeared in the pages and on the covers of the American Legion Monthly between the world wars, so too did those who wrote personal memoirs have to compete with the more vivid images left by such iconic Hollywood films as *All Quiet on the Western Front* and *Sergeant York*. As we inch toward the centennial of the Great War with the last doughboy dying in February 2011, and as we struggle to absorb the contested lessons of World War II, Korea, Vietnam, and America's more recent "small wars"—indeed, at a time when the United States has not drafted anyone into the armed forces for nearly forty years—it is well to reflect and remember when military service was considered part of a citizen's obligation in a democracy, and citizen-soldiers like Robert Patterson gallantly participated in their greatest adventure.

The World War I Memoirs
of Robert P. Patterson

These reminiscences are written for my family. I have tried to tell about the places I covered in the war, the men I came into contact with, the campaigns I participated in. There is little in the narrative that would interest the general reader. Except in one or two instances, I had no adventures that were out of the ordinary. I lived the life of the average officer of a line infantry company.

I have written of events as I remember them fifteen years later. I kept no diary and I have had no papers before me to refresh my memory. I have not tried to give an account of the war in general. In the lines we knew almost nothing of what was going on at other places, and I have restricted the story to the events in which I took a personal part.

Plattsburg

I

When the United States entered the World War in April, 1917, I was working in the law office of Cravath & Henderson. I was then a private in the New York National Guard. When I had come to New York from law school in 1915, I had enlisted in Company I, 7th New York Infantry. There was drilling every Thursday night. In June 1916, the entire National Guard of the country had been mustered into Federal service and had been sent to the Mexican Border because of the threat of war with Mexico. The 7th New York left late in June and spent about five months at McAllen, Texas. These five months covered my military training. I acquired only three things of value: first, a fair knowledge of infantry close-order drill; second, a feeling of sympathy for the ordinary private who marches all day with a pack on his back; and, third, a realization that in the army it is useless to be a kicker. The third idea was the most important. Strange as it may seem to those who have never served in the army, this lesson is actually hard to learn. I had always known of course that obedience was the first duty of a soldier. But to a man who is accustomed to the independence of civil life, the drudgery that always goes with an ordinary soldier's life comes hard, and along with his labors there springs up a spirit of criticizing openly and freely the foolish orders that a soldier constantly is obliged to obey. Petty injustices are of daily occurrence in the military life, and the average man of spirit rankles under them. After some months, however, there comes a feeling that it is useless to kick against the pricks, that no one cares what your opinions may be, that there is nothing you can do about it, and that cheerful and willing obedience costs no more than sullen and halting obedience. When a man really possesses this point of view, he begins to be a soldier.[1]

There are of course limits even here. Wherever I have served, there have always been some officers or non-commissioned officers who were martinets, men whose chief aim seemed to be to show their authority and to harass as constantly as possible those serving under them.[2] In Texas there was a sergeant in our company who took delight in pouncing on soldiers while enjoying themselves off duty and in inventing work for them to do. In

Private Robert Patterson, left, of the Seventh Infantry, New York National Guard, at Camp in McAllen, Texas, July 1916, with inset, Madero, Texas, September 1916. From collection of the Patterson family.

France we had a captain in our regiment who could not bear to see officers or men having a little relaxation. Even the spirit of cheerful obedience does not enable a soldier to grin and bear it with such specimens as these. They are universally hated.[3]

II

Getting back to April, 1917, it seemed to me that I was fit for a commission as lieutenant. While my military training had not amounted to much, it was considerably more than most of my friends had had. The government had recently started the system of an officers' reserve corps, and examinations for commissions in the reserve corps were being held at the Army post on

Panoramic photograph of the Seventh Infantry, New York National Guard, taken at McAllen, Texas, July 4, 1916, during the border crisis with Mexico. From collection of the Patterson family.

Governors Island. One morning in April I went down to Governors Island and presented myself as a candidate for a second lieutenancy in infantry, the lowest commission in existence. As it turned out, the examination was largely a matter of form, and in June, 1917, while I was training in Plattsburg, my commission as second lieutenant of infantry reached me.

At the same time the announcement was made that training camps for men who wished to become officers would be held throughout the country, beginning in May.[4] The instruction was to cover three months and the successful candidates would receive officers' commissions. The camp for New York City men was to be at Plattsburg. I was still enlisted in the 7th New York, which complicated matters for a time; but I succeeded in obtaining from the colonel of the regiment a ninety-day furlough to attend the Plattsburg camp. Under the rule, if I failed to win an officer's commission, I would return to the 7th in my grade of private. Quite a number of my friends in the 7th obtained similar furloughs.

III

The camp opened on May 12, 1917.[5] I will not go into great detail as to what went on there. At first I was in the 8th Company. For the first month the routine work of the soldier was taken up, and at the end of the month the students were allowed to choose which branch they preferred—infantry, cavalry, artillery, or coast artillery. My choice was infantry. In the first place, my only experience was in the infantry, and my commission was in the infantry. In the second place, the infantry was the backbone of the army, the hardest of all the branches of service; and as long as we were in for a war, I felt that I might as well go the limit.

The Ocean and England

I

Our company left Camp Upton on April 12th, 1918. The train took us to New York and without stopping to Boston, where we embarked on S. S. *Karoa* on the 13th.[1]

On board were the Headquarters Company, E Company, Supply Company and Machine Gun Company of our regiment, and also all four companies of the 306th Machine Gun Battalion. The *Karoa* was a small East Indian ship which ordinarily plied between India and Australia. The ship's officers were British and the crew was Hindu. The cabins for us officers were comfortable, but the quarters for the soldiers down below were fearful. This was my first sight of the hardships of war. The overcrowding was beyond belief. Rough tables had been knocked together and placed in the lower decks. The men slept on these tables and under them on the floor, and as many as possible slept in hammocks.[2] There were no bunks of any sort, nor was there sufficient room in the hammocks and on the floor for all of them to lie down. The air down below could be cut with a knife. The *Karoa* was so small that it rocked and tossed continually, which added to the sad state of affairs below.

We sailed from Boston to New York where we lay two days off Staten Island, waiting for the rest of the convoy. Naturally no one was allowed to leave the boat.

The convoy consisted of fully a dozen ships, with a battleship in front for protection. The ships were of all sizes, ours being one of the smallest. They were about half a mile apart and sailed at the same speed, each ship keeping in the same position. This made it appear as if all were standing still and gave a strange effect. The ships were camouflaged with broad streaks of paint zigzagged up and down their sides. It was hard to believe that this made them less visible at a distance.[3]

II

I shared a cabin with Captain George F. Gaston of the 306th Machine Gun Battalion. Every morning a Hindu brought in black coffee and oranges.

Lieutenant Robert P. Patterson at Plattsburg Officers Training Camp, August 1917. From collection of the Patterson family.

The last two months I spent in the 2nd Company at Plattsburg. The work was hard but interesting—work on the rifle range, practice marches, small maneuvers in the field, map-drawing, signaling, conducting company drill, and so on. The climate at Plattsburg was wonderful, with Lake Champlain beside the camp for swimming and sailing. The men at the camp were as fine fellows as could be found anywhere, and some of my warmest friendships date from those days. All in all, I had as good a time for the three months as I have ever known.[6]

A few days before camp closed I had an experience that taught me a lesson of lasting benefit. Captain Goodwin, the instructor of our company, put me in charge of three platoons and told me to march down the Peru road against the other platoon which was on that day under Joe Fogarty. I did not of course know where Fogarty's men were posted. I started out, having put scouts in advance and on the flanks. The scouts on the flanks would come running in, reporting, in error, the presence of the enemy. On each report I would send out a squad or two. When we finally fetched up against Fogarty's position, we had only two or three squads left and could do nothing, to my great embarrassment. Captain Goodwin then gave me a lecture on the wisdom of always keeping men in hand and on the folly of scattering them over the country. Once gone, they can be collected again only with difficulty and delay.

The camp closed on August 15, 1917, and commissions were awarded. In each company (which consisted of about 120 men), 15 commissions as captain, 15 commissions as first lieutenant, and 50 commissions as second lieutenant were given out, as nearly as I can remember. The balance did not receive commissions. I was lucky and got a captain's commission, with orders to report to Camp Upton on September 1st. Some of the new officers were ordered to various other new camps, but the greater part of the men commissioned at Plattsburg were sent to Camp Upton.

Camp Upton

I

Camp Upton was near Yaphank, Long Island, a little place about seventy miles east of New York City.[1] When we reported for duty, the camp site was covered with pine woods, only a dozen or so wooden barracks having been built at that time. The camp was to be the training ground for the 77th Division, to be recruited from the New York drafted men. There was also the Depot Brigade, which was organized to serve as a reservoir of officers and soldiers who would be used to fill up gaps in the Division.

I was assigned to the Depot Brigade and soon found that this assignment was a discouraging one. Although I was nominally in command of a "battalion" of four companies, the companies were "paper" affairs, consisting only of a lieutenant and two sergeants. The lieutenants were from training camp, the sergeants from the regular army. As the drafted men poured into camp, they would be put into the Depot Brigade companies but would remain there for only a few days or weeks. They would then be sent to the regiments of the Division or to other camps. There was a heavy surplus of captains and lieutenants in the Depot Brigade, with very little to do. The quality of the officers was as high as in the organized regiments, and I have often thought how regrettable it was that most of these men never saw service in France, but spent their entire time doing odd jobs around training camps. Most of them were frantic to get transferred into the Division, but only a few succeeded.

I stayed in the Depot Brigade until January, 1918. For a time I worked on preparing a course of work in signaling, but the course was never given. Later I had charge of the conscientious objectors, a group of cranks who were gathered into a barracks in a corner of the camp. They were not in uniform, were not obliged to drill or to work, and were not molested in any way. Every few days we would march three or four of them up to division headquarters, where General J. Franklin Bell, the venerable division commander, would argue with them.[2] I never knew him to bring any of them around, however. The objectors spent most of their time lying on their cots, reading or arguing with one another.[3]

II

I had almost given up hope of ever seeing active service, when one afternoon in January 1918, after four months in the Depot Brigade, I was called to headquarters and received orders to report for duty to the 306th Infantry. I ran all the way to the other end of the camp, where that regiment was located. I believe that I owe this opportunity for service to Major E. Ormonde Power, whom I had known in Plattsburg and who was then a major in the 306th. I reported to the adjutant, Captain Archibald G. Thacher, whose cordiality to me at that time I have never forgotten. He took me over to the Headquarters Company of the 306th, which I was to command. I should now explain in a general way the plan of a division in 1917–1919.

A division consisted of four infantry regiments, three artillery regiments, three machine gun battalions, a regiment of engineers, and smaller bodies of special troops. The infantry was grouped into two brigades of two regiments each. In our brigade the regiments were the 305th and 306th; in the other brigade they were the 307th and 308th. An infantry regiment was made up

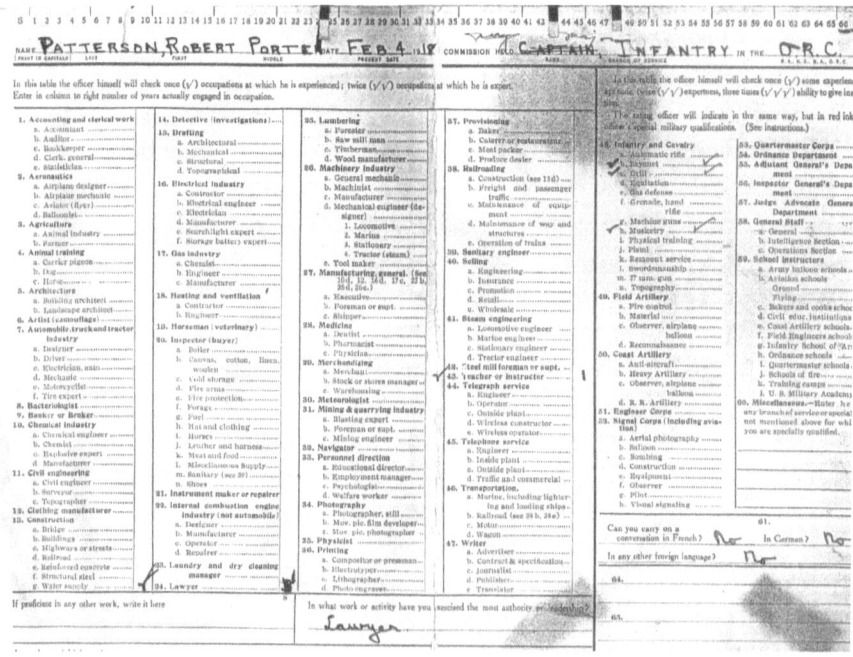

Questionnaire filled out by Robert Patterson in February 1918 for promotion to rank of captain in the AEF. From collection of the Patterson family.

of fifteen companies—twelve rifle companies from A to M, headquarters company, machine gun company, and supply company. The rifle companies, at full strength, had two hundred and fifty men and six officers, the officers being a captain and five lieutenants. Each company had four platoons, with a lieutenant and three sergeants for each platoon. The smallest unit was of course the squad, consisting of a corporal and seven privates. In addition to the rifle strength, a company had a first sergeant, supply sergeant, mess sergeant, four cooks, two mechanics, and a company clerk.

I found myself commanding the Headquarters Company, which at full strength had six lieutenants and three hundred and twenty soldiers. In this company there were five platoons instead of four. (1.) The headquarters platoon consisted of the band, sergeant majors, intelligence section, and others working at regimental headquarters. Seymour Hyde first commanded it, and later Bradford Ellsworth. (2.) The signal platoon was trained in running telephone wires, wigwagging [flag signals], etc. John C. Butler commanded it throughout the war. (3.) The pioneer platoon was supposed to be especially fit for digging trenches, dugouts, etc., more or less like engineers. It was commanded by Jim Cleveland, the fattest officer in the regiment and also one of the best. When we left for France, it was the best-drilled platoon in the entire regiment. (4.) The Stokes mortar platoon carried mortars about four feet long and six inches in diameter which fired a large shell dropped in from the elevated muzzle. Then the shell hit the bottom, the impact touched off a cartridge in the lower end of the shell, and the explosion shot the shell out of the mortar. This weapon had to be elevated at least forty degrees. It had a range of only about six hundred yards. All in all, it was a crude piece of work. This platoon was commanded by Don Antozzi, with Anthony River second in command. Jim Duffy, who had been in the same company at Plattsburg with me and had not won a commission, was a sergeant in this platoon. A man with a finer spirit or with more courage never lived. (5.) The one-pounder platoon had three light guns of 37 millimeter bore. These guns were of French manufacture, had a good range, and were quite accurate. They proved to be effective against machine-gun nests. The guns could be carried by the men for short distances, one man taking the carriage and another carrying the barrel of the gun. Generally, however, the gun was transported on a small carriage drawn by a mule. This platoon was under the command of Lieutenant Elverton C. Crandall, killed during the attack on St. Juvin while aiming one of his guns. He was a very capable and courageous officer.

III

The days now were spent in drilling and in shooting at the rifle range. The winter of 1917–1918 was unusually severe, and the cold interfered considerably with the work at the rifle range. A man's hands would be too cold and stiff to allow careful shooting. The mornings, and also part of the afternoons, were devoted entirely to drilling or rifle work.

I was kept so busy with organizing and equipping the company that at first I became acquainted with but few officers in the regiment. An exception was Father Thomas J. Dunne, the Catholic chaplain. We sat next to one another at mess. He was a man of strong character and unassuming manners, a guileless and open soul. Father Dunne was with the regiment from its organization to the day it was disbanded, and won a place in the heart of every soldier. He never flinched at danger, and his attentions to the wounded and sick never ceased.[4]

The regiment was commanded by Colonel George Vidmer, a cavalry officer in the regular service. He was tireless in whipping the regiment into shape, and in action he was most competent and resourceful. I have rarely known a man with a more alert mind. He had the respect, if not the fear, of officers and men.[5] The adjutant was Captain Archibald G. Thacher, then in his late forties and a prominent admiralty lawyer in New York. He was a thorough gentleman in the true sense—courteous, sympathetic, and understanding, but nevertheless firm and of strong purpose. Later on, as commander of the battalion in which I served, he was an ideal soldier in the field. The 1st battalion was commanded by Major S. Fullerton Weaver, the 2nd by Major Bozeman Bulger who died a year or two ago, the 3rd by Major E. Ormonde Power. The lieutenant colonel, second in command of the regiment, was Garrison McCaskey, an old-timer in the regular army. He left us in France in July 1918 and was succeeded by Lieutenant Colonel Julian Benjamin, who is an uncle of the Benjamins at Garrison, NY, and who frequently visits there. Colonel Benjamin commanded the regiment for about a week before the armistice; he also commanded it for some months after the armistice.

On Washington's Birthday the entire division paraded on Fifth Avenue in a snowstorm.[6] There were of course numerous regimental reviews at Camp Upton. In March the story was passed around that the 77th Division had been reported to the War Department as fit for service in France, and shortly afterward there were plenty of signs that we would sail soon. The weaker men were transferred to the Depot Brigade, the companies were recruited up to full strength; and equipment was issued to the limit. Everyone was given forty-eight hours' furlough. I recall that in the Headquarters Company two men failed to turn up after this furlough. I sent two men, Sergeant Joseph Mercury and Private Patrick Carroll, to New York City to round them up. They came back at the point of the bayonet and remained under guard until we sailed. Both had excellent records later in France and both were killed in action. One of them was beside me when he was struck with a shell, only four or five days before the Armistice. He was carrying some rations for me at the time, as well as a blanket. Neither man had had the slightest intention of deserting when he overstayed furlough; their trouble had been due entirely to excessive drink.[7]

Then we dressed and had breakfast which was quite a hearty meal. The other meals for the officers were on the English plan, too—lunch at noon, tea at five o'clock, and a big dinner at eight-thirty. During the day we had frequent boat-drills, going up to the small boats and rafts on the top deck.

Two days out from Liverpool a fleet of torpedo boats met us and cruised in and out on the watch for submarines. We did not see any "subs," although two of the torpedo boats dropped depth bombs. Whether there were submarines there or whether it was a false alarm we never knew.[4]

After fourteen days on the water we landed at Liverpool. It was a bright Sunday in April, and people on the ferry boats waved and shouted to us. American soldiers were a strange sight to them.[5] We spent the day waiting on the wharves and finally boarded a train. The ride lasted the better part of the night. At the stations we saw many British soldiers who were home on furlough. At one station I recall a wounded "Tommy," who was drunk and was shouting: "I've killed thousands and thousands."

We left the train at Folkestone on the Channel, and spent a day there. I bought a trench coat with a detachable wool lining. The wool lining disappeared when the French rifled our baggage in August, but the coat stayed with me through the war. I slept in it every night and it proved to be most useful. After Folkestone we went to Dover and were put aboard small channel steamers. The voyage across to France took only three hours. It was very rough, however, and for the first time I was seasick. We landed at Calais on April 30, 1918.

A convoy at sea. (Signal Corps. 31017.) From National Archives.

The 77th was, as I recall it, the seventh American division to reach France. The 1st, 2nd, 3rd, 26th, 32nd and 42nd had preceded it. The first three were Regular Army outfits, and the last three were from the National Guard. The 77th was the first of the National Army, the name given to the divisions made up of men taken by conscription.

With the British in Flanders

I

We were with the British for more than a month.

When we landed at Calais, we marched out to a rest "camp" a mile or so from town, where we stayed for three days. Here we turned in our American rifles and received British Lee Enfield rifles, the plan then being that we would fight as part of the British army.[1] We were also issued British helmets and British gas masks, which we kept all through the war. They were practically the same as American helmets and gas masks.

The morning after our arrival I walked into Calais. The British officers with whom I talked seemed utterly discouraged. They could not see why we had landed, when the Germans were about to push the entire British army into the sea. This was just after the disastrous defeats of March and April, 1918, when the Germans nearly finished the war and when Field Marshal Douglas Haig issued his famous "backs to the wall" order. We had been on the water during the April defeats and had heard little about them.[2]

I stood for some time on a bridge over a canal. Canal boats carrying British wounded filled the canal. One after another, they would stop at the wharf, where German prisoners would pick up the stretchers and carry them some distance to the channel steamers bound for home. The wounded never moved or uttered a sound. The procession of canal boats seemed unending. The sight gave me the impression that with all these wounded, there could not be many soldiers left fighting. It was my first contact with the realities of war and had a sobering effect on me for some days.

II

On leaving the Calais rest camp, we took a train as far as Audruicq, a few miles inland. We then marched to a little village called Bonningues, which proved to be our headquarters for most of the time we spent with the British. The soldiers were sheltered in barns and sheds, and the officers found rooms in houses, which was the system whenever troops were billeted in towns. All the infantry regiments of the division were billeted in nearby places.

Bonningues was many miles from the front and was full of civilians. My grasp of the French language was rather poor and I did not get well acquainted with them. The signs of war came from the boom of the guns which we could hear coming from the East every day, and from the German airplanes which frequently came over at night, dropping bombs. No one was hurt, however.[3] Drilling went on under the guidance of British lieutenants and sergeants.

The rations here were British, plenty of tea, jam, and cheese. The men did not take kindly to the tea and missed the coffee which is supplied to the American soldier at every meal.

I found that as captain of the Headquarters Company, under the British system, I was given a horse. My riding was nothing to boast of, but I had a pleasant time on the animal riding around the country.

III

We had been in France about two weeks when the captains and first sergeants were ordered to spend five or six days at the British front, to see the way affairs were managed there. First Sergeant Morrell Smith of the Headquarters Company went with me. We rode most of the day on a London bus, passing through St. Omer and Doullens. Late in the afternoon we approached the front south of Arras, passing through the heavy artillery and then the light artillery. Then we came to ruined villages full of reserve infantry, where we left the bus and proceeded on foot. I was struck by the youthful appearance of the infantry. They seemed to be boys of seventeen or eighteen. The men I had seen behind the lines were full grown and seasoned. The artillerymen were also men in their twenties and thirties. But the "PBIs" of the British Army ("poor bloody infantry") had been shot to pieces so many times in three long years of fighting that the general run of infantrymen consisted of young fellows recently sent over from "Blighty."[4]

We passed the night in a ruined chateau which served as division headquarters. The general was a tired sort of man, quite pleasant and courteous. The next morning we walked up to brigade headquarters, in a shack nearer the front, and from there we went up a road to battalion headquarters where we were to stay.

Battalion headquarters was in a deep dugout, near where the village of Boisleux had once stood. I had never before seen and I never later saw devastation equal to that on the British front. There was literally nothing left of the houses where Boisleux had been. A wall over two feet high was not to be seen in the village. Everything had been leveled to the ground and battered into dust and loose stones. In the German lines opposite was what was left of a place known as Boyelles.

A long stair took us down to the dugout. British soldiers were lying on the steps in the dark. It seemed better to me to stay up on the ground, where it was warm and bright, but it was not long before I changed my point of view. The dugout itself was very damp and dark except for the candles, but it was large and deep enough to be safe. It had four or five rooms. I was told that it had formerly been used as a division headquarters, at a time when the lines were further forward, and this accounted for its being of such good size.

The battalion was of the Royal Fusiliers. A lieutenant-colonel was in command, with three or four lieutenants on his staff. The battalion surgeon was an American from the Middle West. I have forgotten the names of these officers. The rations in the dugout were first-class—far better than we ever had in our own lines later—and there was always plenty of whisky.

A young lieutenant took me up to the front as soon as I had dropped my things and had become acquainted. A short distance forward the communication trenches began. We passed some support trenches, with soldiers in them here and there, and continued on to the front-line trench. Here I saw my first dead man in the war, a corporal who had just been shot through the head with a bullet. The day was a quiet one, however, with little shooting. The soldiers, almost all of them young boys, were standing or sitting about, taking things easy. The trenches zigzagged up and down, with bays twenty feet long or so, like this: (see below, Map 1).

We looked out over the parapet toward the German lines one hundred yards away, but could see nothing moving. I remember an amusing incident on our way back. As we were passing the support trenches, a captain, obviously up from the ranks, called to us. He was in a little hole in the side of a trench; the hole was his headquarters and was large enough for two or three

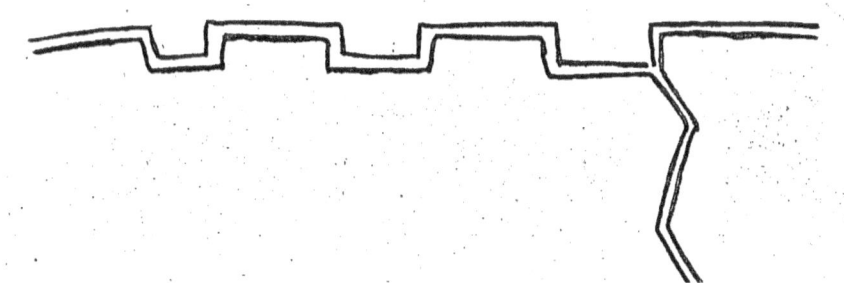

Map 1. Patterson's sketch of trenches in British Sector, July 1918.

men. He invited me down to have tea, and I accepted. He had a pail with chips of wood in it, and he was blowing through holes in the pail to make the wood burn. Inside there was a smaller pail which held the tea. The wood was smoking badly, causing the captain to cough and swear in Cockney. Finally he succeeded in getting the tea hot. While we sat drinking it, two or three machine guns nearby opened up quite a steady fire. The afternoon had been quiet. I put down my cup and started up.[5] The captain told me to sit down and "tyke it easy." I replied that there must be a German attack or some sort of trouble. "Tyke it easy; it's nothing at all," he said. "What are they doing all that shooting for, then?" I asked. "This is tea time in the British army," he said.[6] "Didn't you see me coughing and blowing away at that bloody pail? Those machine-gunners have water in the jacket of their guns, and they are shooting just to warm it up. When it is hot, they will draw it off and have their bloody tea."[7]

He went on to explain how everyone had the advantage over the "PBI" ("Poor Bloody Infantry"), he did not see why he ever went in for the "PBI," etc., with many references to "bloody" this and "bloody" that. I did not put much stock in the story about the machine gunners, but nevertheless it was a good story.[8]

The next day we went up to the front again. The Germans were dropping "minnies" (*minnenwerfers*) along the front, at the rate of about one a minute.[9] These were large heavy shells that were fired from a short mortar and came down from high in the air. Most of them missed the trench, either falling short or going over. The noise of the explosion was terrific, and the hole made was a big one. The "minnies" could be seen as they dropped, and the soldiers were dodging around the bays to escape them. One dropped in a bay not far away where two men were sleeping. We went there and found a large hole where the trench had been. What was left of the two men was put into a sack. The wooden parts of their rifles had been blown to bits, and the steel parts stood alone, twisted and bent beyond recognition. This was my first sight at close range of what high explosives would do.

On the way back we were crossing a large open field when several shrapnel burst in the air above us. I did not feel alarmed at first. Then the young lieutenant with me said we had better run for it, and we lit out for the battalion dugout. The shells continued after us and I "got the wind up," as the British used to say. By the time we reached the dugout I was fit to be tied. After I had sat down where it was safe, the thought came to me that more than a million men had been killed in the war and that the loss of life to me would not be worse than their loss was to them. I never again got into the state of mind I had been in during that shelling.[10]

At night there would be more activity. Lights and flares would make the place as bright as day, and the shooting would increase. The Canadian Corps was just north of us, and at night there was a great clatter along their front. The lieutenant colonel explained to me that there was much more fighting there, with raids and patrols by the Canadians. His own boys were just over from home and were too raw to stand that sort of thing. I saw several of the Canadians along the road in daytime and understood the difference. They were mature men, of considerable experience and sure of themselves.

One day I went back with an artillery officer to where the field artillery was located. Going through a field, I saw a dozen or so graves and glanced at one. It bore the name "Lionel Harvard," lieutenant in the Grenadier Guards, with a date of death only a week or two before. He was a descendant of John Harvard or of his brother and had been in Harvard College when I was at law school. It was an odd thing that I should have seen his grave, he being almost the only man in the British army I had ever seen or heard of before the war.[11]

I stayed with the British battalion four or five days. I lost my bedding roll coming back from the lines. It had been put on the ration cart the night before and never turned up again. I still had some stuff, however, in a canvas bag I had left at Bonningues. On returning to the company, I found the training and drilling still going on. The pioneer Stokes mortars and cannon platoons had been sent away to nearby towns to attend schools, and there was little for me to do. It was at this time that I first asked the colonel for a transfer to a rifle company. I had a feeling that in fighting my place as captain of the headquarters company was unimportant and that I would prefer to see the war through in command of an ordinary line company. I did not get a transfer for some time, however.

IV

In May we had a memorable time on a three-day practice maneuver known in our regiment as the "Battle of Watten."[12] The affair was hopelessly bungled from the start. The orders were confused, and the men were still soft. The result was a general collapse. We started marching in winter equipment, with heavy packs. The day was hot. By noon all kinds of surplus stuff that the men had brought with them from the United States had been thrown away, and the straggling was bad. By the middle of the afternoon, fully half of the men had fallen out along the road, nursing their feet, looking for water or just lying down exhausted. Staff officers dashed up and down in automobiles and side-cars, shouting orders and threats, with no one paying any attention to them. When we finally arrived near Watten at dark, some companies had not over twenty men. We fooled around for a day and then marched back. I recall seeing Charles "Pat" O'Brien, a lieutenant in C Company, on the return march. He was one of the best officers in the regiment, a fine big Irishman. He was marching beside the C Company kitchen and told me he was under arrest. A colonel on the division staff had seen him marching with his helmet in his hand instead of on his head, and had placed him under arrest.

As we approached Bonningues I stopped to let my horse get a drink at a brook. He waded in and began to fill up. I was not paying much attention to him until I felt myself going down. The horse was on his knees in the brook. I jumped just as he started to roll over in the water, missed the bank and got a good wetting. My equipment was tied on the rear of the saddle and was so soaked with water and plastered with mud that I had to abandon it and stock up again. I traded this horse to a British officer for another on the march to the trains at Anvin, but got little use of the new horse as I was transferred to F Company shortly afterward. All officers of rifle companies marched on foot.

Early in June we were informed that we were not going in with the British after all, but were to take over a quiet front down near Switzerland. Our

French 77-mm field gun. (111-Signal Corps 39958.) From National Archives.

American rifles were brought from Calais and reissued to us. We marched south for five days (the marching was well done this time), and took the railroad at Anvin.

The crowding of soldiers into the cars beat anything I had ever seen. Each freight car was supposed to hold forty men, which was fitting them in very tight; but in fact most cars held fifty. None could lie down, and many could not even sit down on the floor. The choice places were in the doors, where men could sit and hang their legs out. The officers were fairly comfortable in compartments on ordinary French passenger cars. We were on the train three days.[13]

V

The British army was an army that had maintained its discipline despite the long years of fighting. The men saluted smartly and kept their uniforms clean. On the march their ranks were well closed up. I would see British wagons parked in a field. As soon as one would come in from the muddy road it would be cleaned and polished, although the men knew that in an hour or two it would be on the road again covered with mud. I found later that the French, although good soldiers, were not much on discipline. The saluting was very casual. A French company on the march would be spread up and down the road for a mile, each man taking his own time about it. A French wagon-train on the road looked like a caravan of gypsies, with bundles tied here and there and no effort made to keep the wagon in orderly condition. Nevertheless the French fought very well, as everyone knows.

The Baccarat Sector

I

It was June 5, 1918, when we left our old quarters up in Flanders near St. Omer, and we arrived behind the Baccarat sector on June 12. We relieved the 42nd (Rainbow) Division on June 18. We remained in this sector until early in August.

The Baccarat sector was a quiet front where tired troops or green troops held the line. Baccarat itself was about ten miles in the rear and was division headquarters. It is a city well down toward the Swiss frontier, in the foothills of the Vosges.

On leaving the railroad at Charmes, we marched to a small place near Rambervillers and stayed there for three or four days. The name of the village I have forgotten. We then proceeded by night to Baccarat, passing in the dark the 165th Infantry (old 69th New York) which was being relieved. Many of our boys had friends in this Irish outfit, and it was amusing to hear them calling out: "What company is this?" "Do you know Kelly in B Company?" And so on most of the night.

We went forward from Baccarat several miles to Brouville, where the headquarters of the 306th was located.[1] The Stokes mortar platoon and the one pounder platoon moved on into the front line at Ancerviller, where I looked them over that night. The front was very quiet. No Man's land was half a mile wide, and not a shot was fired all day. Many of the men lived in the houses of the town, where they made themselves comfortable. Cooked rations were regularly sent forward. All in all, it was a well-conducted and easy-going war at that spot.

Back in Brouville I had almost nothing to do for a week or more. I again approached the colonel for a transfer to a rifle company, to get more active service. To my great joy he ordered me to go to F Company, Captain Charles E. Johnstone of that company being shifted to Headquarters Company at the same time. So Johnstone and I changed jobs, and on July 5 I went up to take over my new company, then stationed in support between Montigny and Ancerviller behind G Company. Except for a period of three weeks just before the Armistice when I commanded the 2nd battalion, all of my subsequent service in the war was as captain of F Company. Naturally I came to the conviction that it was the best and most dependable company in the regiment.

II

The 2nd battalion was then in command of Major Thacher. He was without doubt one of the best officers in the entire division—cool, quick in coming to decisions, and always well posted on the condition of affairs. He knew the points of his officers, too, and had the faculty of picking out the right one for a particular job. E Company was commanded by Captain Bennett, a regular army officer who did not remain long with us. G Company was under Captain Charles M. Bull, Jr., and H Company was under Captain Julius O. Adler. Both were excellent officers and the best of fellows. Bull had the devotion and loyalty of his soldiers to a marked degree. Later, when we were on the Vesle, my men picked up a runner from his company who was badly wounded by machine gun fire. While we were binding him up that night in my hole, I tried to cheer him up and told him that he would soon be home. "I don't want to go home," he said, "I want to go back to Captain Bull. He's good enough for me." As long as Bull was on hand, the men in G Company had confidence that everything would turn out all right.

Adler was a natural-born soldier, one of the sort that instinctively does the right thing in a pinch.[2] He had the hardness of steel when resolution was required, and did not know what fear was. He was a strict disciplinarian, and H Company was one of the strongest companies in the regiment throughout the war.

The lieutenants in F Company were Michael J. Hayes, Ralph McCarthy, and Richard R. Blazer. John J. Riordan of M Company was also with the company when I joined it, but he was on temporary duty and soon returned to his own company. McCarthy returned to the United States early in August. Blazer was with the company throughout, except for a month in the Argonne when he was attached to H Company. Both were capable officers.

Hayes served with the company from its organization until his death on October 14, 1918, in the attack on St. Juvin. It is not too much to say that he was the life and soul of the company, the finest soldier I have ever seen. There was not a flaw in him. He had a grand physique, six feet one in height and weighing 190 pounds. His strength and endurance were remarkable. I have seen him carry for hours, without apparent effort, the packs of three or four exhausted soldiers. His personality won the hearts of officers and men alike, and he had a smile for everyone. He never swore or had a hard word for anyone. If a man disappointed him, which was rare, he did not resort to abuse. He was the only officer I knew who could talk earnestly to men on patriotism, love of country, devotion to duty and such topics, and really inspire them. He was a devout Catholic, and spent quite a bit of his spare time reading a New Testament which he always kept in his pocket. He often told me of the comfort he got from prayer. His courage was of the bold, impetuous kind that once in, risked all; but the thing that made Hayes such a wonderful soldier was the combination of this headlong courage with an excellent mind for planning and foreseeing developments. In the lines he would spend hours in figuring out the way to handle any emergency and in impressing his plan upon his men, but when the time came to act, he moved like a flash. The influence of Hayes made every man in the company twice the soldier he otherwise would have been, and I believe that he exercised a lasting influence for good in the lives of most of them. He was a great developer of men. He would take a rather average private and make him into a capable corporal or sergeant. His death on the field was the one occasion in the war when everyone made no secret of his sorrow.

The first sergeant when I joined was James A. Cassidy. He was sent back to the United States in August to train recruits, and Frank Taylor was made first sergeant. Taylor was later sent back to receive a commission, and Edward F. McLoughlin became first sergeant. McLoughlin had been in the army twenty-five years and was a seasoned, steady soldier. The mess sergeant at first was George F. Jones, then Morris Brenner, and finally Peter Finucane. Finucane was a great, all-around soldier; in the lines or at the kitchen he never failed us. The supply-sergeant was William T. Slover. Among the line sergeants were Lo Bono, Joseph A. Faucher, and Joseph E. Zimmerman of the 1st platoon, William F. Hennessy, Michael Connolly and William R. Stewart of the 2nd, Charles J. Johnson and Henry J. Breitwieser of the 3rd, and Frederick W. Peterson of the 4th. As things would happen to them, the list of sergeants would change.

Hayes told me that we were short of corporals. We promoted several, and I obtained the transfers of Privates Patrick Carroll and Thomas Murphy from Headquarters Company, making them corporals. Their later records proved the wisdom of this. Both were badly wounded later on. At the same time I obtained the transfer of Joe Madden from Headquarters Company. He was my striker [enlisted man performing extra duty for an officer] until he was gassed in August. Armando Salvini thereafter acted as striker until about the time of the armistice when Madden returned and recovered the job.

III

In the Baccarat sector the stay of a battalion in front was ten days, in support ten days, and back in reserve ten days. All of these tours of duty were easy in that sector. Except for a few shells a day, there was no shooting. The day I joined I was walking with Hayes to the support trenches occupied by the first platoon, which was across a little valley from the others, when we heard a shot nearby. We ran toward the noise and found Privates David Lowenthal and Halter sitting in a trench. One of them had fired at a rat and the bullet had passed between the legs of the other. Halter was later wounded and captured, dying in a German hospital.

After a few days spent pleasantly in the Montigny position, we were moved back to reserve, near Brouville. This was in a camp with barracks, which the soldiers called Mud Camp. It was a good place despite its name, and we had a good time there, drilling, practicing with hand grenades, playing baseball, with a one-day leave to Baccarat. There was a celebration on July 14th, Bastille Day, in which some neighboring French companies participated.

After the customary ten days, the 2nd Battalion moved up to the support position at Reherry. This was practically as easy as in reserve. Reherry was full of civilians carrying on as usual, and most of F Company lived in houses or in barracks. The only unpleasant feature was that we were obliged to furnish large details of men to the engineers for the digging of dugouts and trenches. As proved always to be the case, the engineers only directed the job. Even the engineer privates were spared from actual digging. The heavy manual work was done by the infantry. The credit went to the engineers of course. I found that this was typical of a point of view in the army, whereby infantry soldiers are regarded as unskilled laborers available for doing all sorts of heavy labor for special troops—digging or repairing roads under the engineers, carrying machine guns and ammunition for machine gunners, and so forth. Although this sort of thing was of course proper in emergencies, its prevalence as a regular practice was harmful. Infantry soldiers under fighting conditions have the hardest task and no efforts should be spared to build up their morale. If, in addition to their own work, they are treated as beasts of burden for other troops, and this too at times when they are supposed to be at rest, the effect upon their spirit is unquestionably bad.

IV

It was now late in July and news had come in of the Allied counteroffensive on the Marne. Through French newspapers we heard of the Marne,

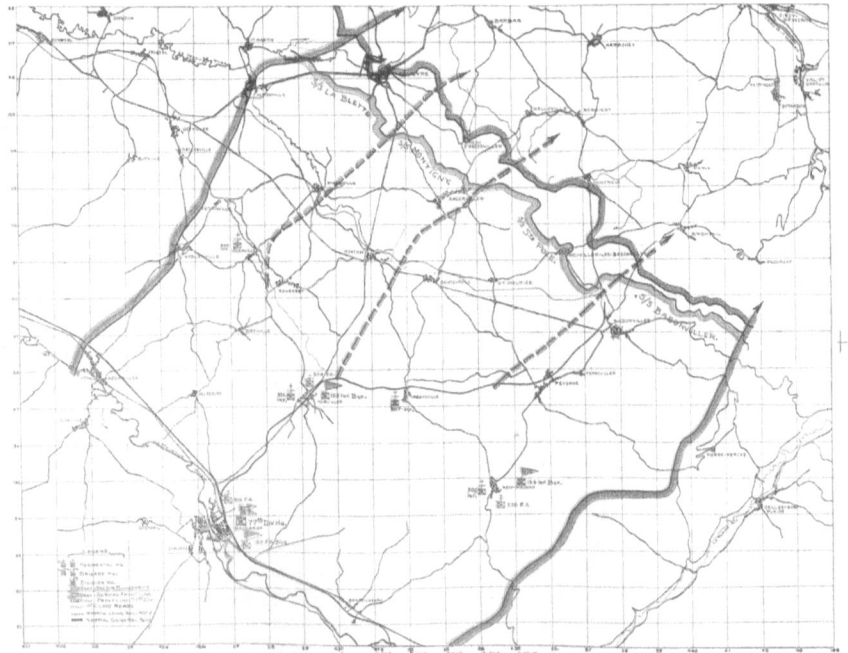

Map 2. 77th Division movements in the Baccarat Sector, July 1918. From Julius Adler, *History of the Seventy-seventh Division.*

the Ourcq and the Vesle, Chateau-Thierry, Fere-en-Tardenois, Sergy, and Flames. We had been in France for three months, and everyone was eager to serve in an active sector. Our hopes were realized when the 77th Division was relieved by the 37th, the Ohio National Guard. We made a long night march back to the rear, resting at a French village during the day. This was followed by two more night marches. These moves in the dark were to avoid observation by enemy airplanes. All night marches are alike. At the start the men are in high spirits, singing, laughing, and cracking jokes. By midnight the gaiety begins to die down, and by two or three o'clock it has vanished. The only sound then is the shuffle of feet and curses at the stones and ruts in the road. If it is raining, nothing is more cheerless than a night march. But there is less straggling at night than in the day. For one thing, it is cooler. And then the feeling of not being able later to find the company if one falls out is stronger in the dark and keeps a man on his feet.

We arrived in the neighborhood of the railhead at Blainville, where we were to take the trains, and stayed two or three days under shelter tents in a forest. On the night of August 4th we entrained, the men being packed forty to a freight car and the officers riding in compartments on passenger cars. After two days on the train, we detrained at Coulommiers, a place not far from Paris. This clearly meant that we were destined for active service on the Marne front. The train on which we had travelled held L Company and Supply Company as well as the 2nd Battalion, and we had a lively time getting the wagons of the Supply Company off the flat cars in the dark. The work of unloading was directed by Tony Czak, then a lieutenant in the Supply Company and a remarkable character. Czak had been in the army for twenty years, most of the time a sergeant. He spoke with a strong German accent but managed to swear in excellent English. He had the gift of telling trivial stories in the most entertaining fashion. He was full of energy and could get an amazing amount of work out of soldiers. After the armistice he was made captain of H Company. I was thrown with him a great deal and never had a dull moment in his company. When the army was restored to a peace basis, he was reduced to his old rank of sergeant, was later retired, and died some years subsequently.

The Vesle Sector

I

By early August the Germans had retreated from the Marne and had dug in along the Vesle between Soissons and Rheims. There the lines stayed during August. Our division and the 28th Division confronted them, and a good deal of fighting of a local character took place. For the most part this consisted of attacks by companies or battalions of Americans and counterattacks by the Germans. Our losses in these affairs were generally heavy and there was no compensating advantage beyond the experience gained.[1]

Upon leaving the trains at Coulommiers we marched a short distance north and went into camp for a day at Boissy le Chatel. We were then to be moved to the front in trucks. Some twenty or thirty weak men in each company were left behind to march up on foot. The rest of the regiment was loaded on trucks which carried us through Chateau-Thierry and on up to Fere-en-Tardenois.[2] Just north of Fere is the Forest of Nesle where we were dropped. We moved into the woods and bivouacked for the night. It was understood that the 2nd Battalion was to be in the front, with E and F Companies out across the Vesle. The other two battalions were to be in support and in reserve.

II

The next morning, August 11th, Major Thacher and the four captains went up toward the Vesle by automobile. At Loupeigne we were directed up to the headquarters of a French regiment at Mont Notre Dame, a little village south of the Vesle. This was the regiment that we were to relieve. We found the headquarters in a cave on a hill behind Mont Notre Dame and were warmly welcomed. After eating a first-class dinner at headquarters, Bennett of E Company and I put on French overcoats and helmets and each with a French guide went forward to the river. The day was hot and the overcoats uncomfortable. As we neared the river, crouching over so as not to be seen, there were many bodies of dead Frenchmen and Americans in the grass, and the odor was very bad. A dozen times I said audibly "whew" and *"très mauvais.*" The guide said never a word, until finally we came upon a dead German. Then he turned and assured me that all the smell came from the German: "*Pas des Français; pas des Americains; seulement le sale Boche.*"

We crossed the Vesle on a small foot-bridge held in place by stakes driven into the bed of the stream, stopped a few minutes at the French battalion headquarters in a little hollow, and then crawled some little distance forward and to the right, to the headquarters of the company that I was to relieve. The French captain there was most cordial and pointed out the situation of his company. I will describe the place.

It was along the railroad tracks half a mile west of Bazoches, a village on the north bank of the Vesle. The Vesle was two or three hundred yards in the rear; the railroad tracks were in a deep cut here, and the main line of defense was in the cut.[3] North of the tracks there was a wide, level field. The advance posts were in little shallow trenches in this field, some three hundred yards beyond the tracks. South of the tracks lay a lagoon, with a patch of woods just behind it. The company headquarters was in a little dugout between the lagoon and the tracks and connected with the lagoon by a short communication trench two or three feet deep. The sketch given below will give an idea of the position, as well as of the disposition of the three platoons of F Company in occupying it.

III

Upon my return to Mont Notre Dame we all went back to the Forest of Nesle by automobile and started getting the companies ready for the march up. Hayes had been talking to the men and all were eager for the front.[4] It was after dark when the battalion moved out for the rather long march to Mont Notre Dame where the French guides were to meet us and take us into position. On passing through Fere, the captains persuaded Major Thacher to take us up by automobile to regimental headquarters at Mont Notre Dame. There we received final orders from the colonel, and Bull and Adler were sent back to join the marching column. Thacher, Bennett, and I lay down in the ditch behind the town, where the French guides were waiting. As the night wore on, the guides got impatient and finally said that it was too late to cross the Vesle and make the relief. The troops came up about three o'clock in the morning and were led down a little road to the east, the plan being to lie in position there and make the relief the next night. As we were leaving the main road a heavy shelling from the enemy came down on the place where the troops were. This was the first serious fire for most of the men, and there was some confusion. There were casualties in the other

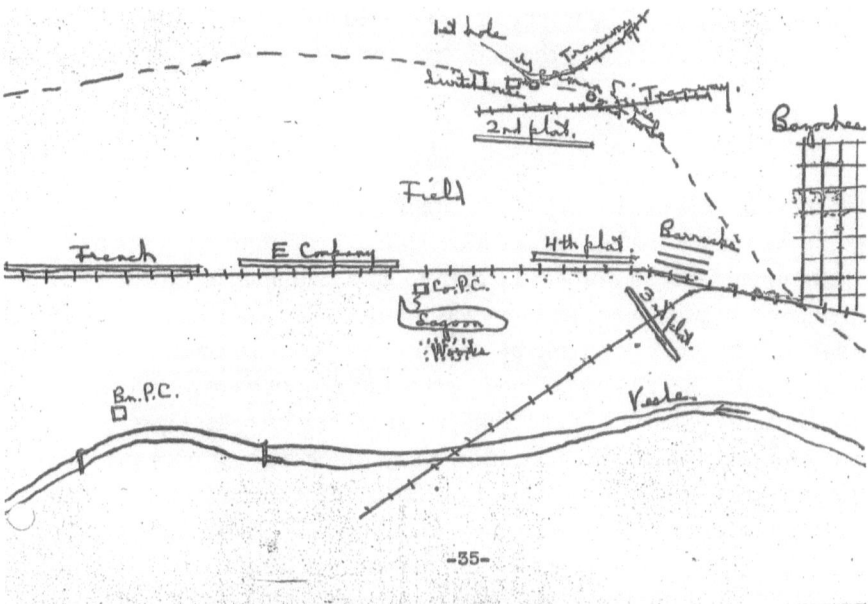

Map 3. Disposition of forces near Bazoches, France, August 13–14, 1918.

companies, but F Company got through without loss, the men lying in the ditches beside the road.[5]

We waited all day under cover and prepared to move out in the evening. The men had two days' reserve rations in their packs and ate one day's rations here. (The reserve ration for one day was a can of corned beef and two boxes of hard tack.) We left our packs (except the rations) in this place and posted a man to guard them. Apprehending that it would be hard to get rations in the position north of the Vesle, I sent a squad to Mont Notre Dame to find more reserve rations and have them ready to pass out to the men as we marched through on the relief. Almost the entire first platoon was taken from us to carry in machine gun ammunition. Sergeant Lo Bono, Corporal Carroll, Private Duffy, and one or two others of that platoon remained and were attached to the 2nd platoon. The men on the ammunition detail never joined us in the position. They wandered around with the machine gunners and finally returned to the position behind Mont Notre Dame. Another mishap was that on the way in, half of the 4th platoon wandered off in the dark and never reached the place. The platoons were led separately by guides in single file, and when the Germans sent up star shells it was necessary for all to drop down and remain motionless while the light lasted. During these waits each man was to keep hold of the man in front, thus keeping the connection; but someone was inattentive on this occasion and the rear half of the platoon lay still after the front half had moved on. So we had only two and a half platoons on the spot—the 2nd, 3rd, and half of the 4th.

IV

We moved out about ten in the evening of August 12. I was in front with the guide. When we reached Mont Notre Dame, I saw nothing of the men sent ahead for rations, so I ordered a man to go ahead and find them while the file halted and fell out. The town was being shelled, but we had no trouble. At this point the major came up and ordered me to proceed with the relief without delay, which I was obliged to do. The rations were missed, however; for the last three days of our "trek" north of the Vesle there was nothing to eat. I might say here that the ration party which we sent back the night of the 13th procured water but had insufficient time to get food; the party on the 14th was gassed in Mont Notre Dame; no party was sent on the 15th because a relief was expected but did not materialize.

We crossed the Vesle on foot bridges and made our way forward, with frequent stops on account of star shells. The French departed for the rear upon our appearance, except a few sergeants who remained a day longer, and we were in the front on an active sector, close up against the enemy. As shown on the sketch [map 3, above], the 2nd platoon under Hayes, about forty men, was out in front of the tracks. The place was a wretched one, taken over from the French. The trench was only waist deep. The barbed wire in front was merely low wire on hoops and could be easily jumped. The place was wholly exposed to observation and fire from the German posts one hundred yards away, and during the day it could not be reached from the rear. This trench out in front weakened the main position on the tracks, as it interfered with what would otherwise have been a good field of fire. I believe that the trench was not occupied by the companies that took this post later.

The twenty men in the fourth platoon who came in were under Blazer and were posted on the railroad near Bazoches. They had holes dug in on the front side of the cut. The place was fairly strong, but was exposed to an enfilading fire from the enemy near the railroad station at Bazoches. The third platoon was split into two parts, one under Sergeant Johnson and one under Sergeant Breitwieser, and was in small trenches in the field, posted to cover the right flank. I was in the lagoon, along with a squad of pioneers under Corporal Hillen and some machine gunners.

At this place there were many dead Americans, most of them from the 47th Infantry and a few from the 39th Infantry. These were regiments in the 4th Division, which had made unsuccessful attacks on Bazoches.

There was heavy machine gun fire during the night from Bazoches and the region to the west of it.[6] We had several casualties in the 2nd platoon, among them Private Charles W. Wogatzke killed and Sergeant William F. Hennessy wounded. I ran out to the 2nd platoon and found the men there busily firing away. Hayes told me that at first the men had been nervous under the close firing, but had steadied down as soon as he gave the order to open fire and keep it up. The rifles and the Chauchats were banging away when I arrived.

On my return to the tracks I ran fast so as to get in between the star shells. When not more than thirty feet from the tracks, I was fired on point-blank. I dropped down and shouted, but two more shots came. I continued shouting and heard an answer. I then came in and found that a squad of E Company had been shooting at me in the belief that I was a German. One of these men was Edward Toomey, whom I have often seen since the war. I explained to the group that F Company had a large post out in front, that there would be considerable traffic back and forth, and that they must take care about firing. This was one of the closest shaves I ever had.

V

The next day was quiet except for *minnenwerfers*. I spent the morning sleeping. When I came out, I saw the corpse of a soldier brought in from the 2nd platoon. They told me that it was Stephen Mikowski. The man had no identification tag. He had been shot in the face and was unrecognizable to me. So I ordered him buried near the lagoon and put down Mikowski as killed in the casualty report. It was a week or so later that I found in talking to Hayes that Mikowski was all right and that the dead man was Wogatzke. I made a corrected report at once, but Mikowski was reported killed back home.[7]

In the morning the enemy began a bombardment with *minnenwerfers* from Bazoches. The first few landed in the patch of woods just behind the lagoon. We thought that the position in the lagoon had been spotted and that soon the range would be corrected and we would be in trouble. They continued landing in the woods, however, and it was evident that the Germans thought there was a body of men there. The trees were thoroughly shattered by afternoon, but no loss was sustained by us.

The night of the 13th was active. Machine guns began to bark up and down the German lines, and we had some men wounded in the 4th platoon from bullets that came down the track from Bazoches.

Just before dark there was a long burst of fire out near Hayes's platoon, followed by cries for help. A little later some men came in carrying a French sergeant who had been staying with Hayes. (It was the custom on a relief for one or two men of the relieved platoon to remain for a day with the new outfit, so as to make them familiar with the place.) The man was shot through both legs. He had been protesting against our shooting the previous night on the ground that it would bring about an attack and had left the trench before dark, evidently in order to get out before the expected attack.

Bullets passing near a person have a strange effect. Sometimes they merely whistle as they go by. But often they make a sharp crack in the air, giving the impression that they have been fired from only a few feet off, whereas in fact the men who have fired them are three or four hundred yards away.

Soon after dark I sent runners to the platoons to have a ration party made up, but it was after midnight before all of the men were assembled in the lagoon. Water was even more important than food. The party of twenty men, under Corporal Patrick J. Carroll, set out for Mont Notre Dame where the kitchen was located, each carrying several canteens. They returned just before dawn, with water which they had procured at a spring on the way back but without rations. They had estimated that if they proceeded on to the kitchen it would be daylight before they could get back.

VI

I now come to the greatest adventure of my life. During the night I received a message from battalion headquarters to the effect that the enemy was believed to be retiring to the Aisne. I immediately sent out a patrol of three men under Sergeant Breitwieser. The patrol was discovered and got back with difficulty. About three in the morning on August 14th, I noticed that the German machine gun fire which had been heavy ceased abruptly. The notion took hold of me that the heavy fire had been to cover a retirement and that the enemy had gone. After daylight I picked up a rifle and with Corporal Carroll and Corporal Robert A. Straub walked in the field along the edge of the tracks, ready to jump down to the tracks if fired upon. Nothing happened. We then went to look over some old barracks that stood near Bazoches in front of the tracks, but found nothing there. My idea as to the Germans having withdrawn was now a conviction, and after a short delay we walked out across the field to Hayes's trench. He felt that the enemy was close at hand but could not account for our being able to walk about without drawing fire. I told him that we were going out in front as far as the hills, that when we drew fire we would drop down and crawl back, and that then we would advance the whole company. It was about seven in the morning when we started out. There is no doubt in the world that I was exceedingly careless in this matter. Hayes proved to be right.

With Carroll and Straub I walked out about one hundred and fifty yards, crossing over a tramway and passing several dead Germans. We had unknowingly passed through the hostile advanced posts. I then noticed a small switch-house to our left and rear and turned toward it. The sketch

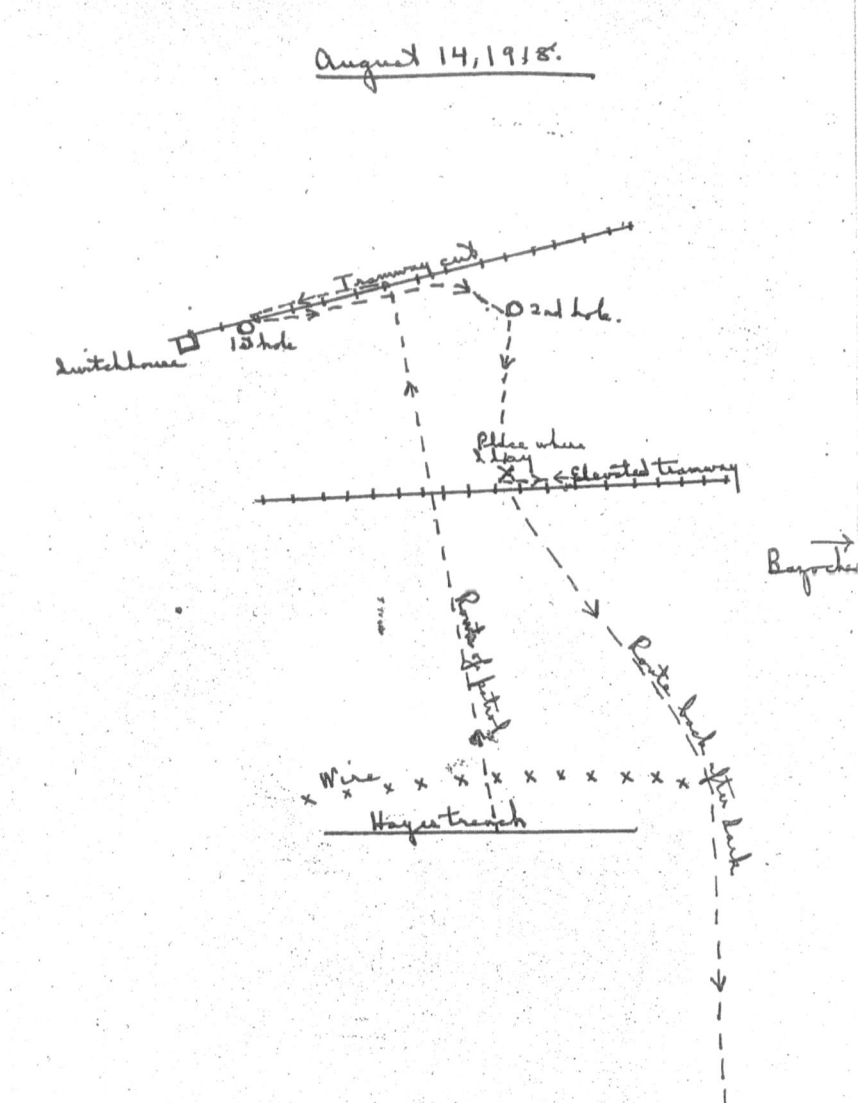

Map 4. Patterson's map of the firefight with Germans just west of Bazoches on August 14, 1918.

of the position near Bazoches shows the location of the house, the German holes, and the tramways. We were walking along a tramway cut into the ground. Just before reaching the house I saw a shell-hole on the side of the tramway cut. In it were five or six Germans, one standing up in the middle and the others lying down. I was no more than twelve feet from them. The boy standing up saw me at the same time. I brought up my rifle, tried to shoot, and found that it was locked. I pushed the lock and fired, hitting the man in the head. His little round cap sailed up and up. A moment later I heard a crash behind me, from Carroll's gun. I glanced around and saw him putting on his bayonet, and bringing the gun up. He later told me that his gun had jammed after firing and he could not extract the empty cartridge. I called out to run and we dashed down the tramway. Nothing more was seen or heard of this group of Germans. We could have captured the whole group if I had not commenced to fire; whether we could have brought them off to our lines is another matter.

I realized that the course we were on would not bring us to our own lines, and we jumped out. Just then we struck another shell-hole full of Germans. It was evident that we had passed between their advanced posts and now were striking them on our way back. I can account for our safety in crossing No Man's Land only by assuming that the Germans had been busy all night and did not expect any trouble in broad daylight. I stood on the edge of the hole and was about to shoot the man standing in the middle when I noticed two men lying asleep right under my feet. I dropped the muzzle and fired, hitting one of them in the back. I then called to the corporals to make for our lines and turned myself to go. I could see Hayes standing in his trench. After one or two steps I decided to cover the retreat of the others, ran back, and fired from the hip into the shell-hole. Two or three were now up and shooting. I think that I did not hit any, and I know that they did not hit me, although we were firing face to face. The bolt of the rifle would not go in and it dawned on me that the magazine was empty. I had no time to reload from the clips in my belt. I threw the rifle down at the men and ran for our lines. I had covered perhaps thirty feet when two or three bullets whistled by. I decided that to run farther without being struck would be hopeless, threw up my arms as if hit, and fell in the grass.

It was unfortunate that I had fallen on the German side of a tramway elevated one or two feet above the field; otherwise I could have crawled on through the grass. As it was, I would first be obliged to jump the track. I lay motionless at the foot of the bank, hugging the ground and hoping that if the enemy saw me they would take me for dead, my nose was pressed into the sand, and was raw; the clips in the cartridge belt made dents in my chest.

From time to time the Germans fired a machine gun from the shell-hole in front of which I lay, and the vibration would ring on my helmet. They were firing not at me but over the tramway at our post. A dozen times I had made up my mind to take a chance and jump the tramway. Then a volley would come which would have finished me, and I would decide that it was better where I was.[8]

This went on for an hour or so, when I heard four or five heavy explosions over near the shell-hole, followed by shouts and shots from the Germans. I supposed that the explosions were from rifle grenades that the men in Hayes's trench had fired. There were groans from the shell-hole for an hour or more. What had happened was that Hayes with four men had come out to rescue me. When he saw me fall he thought I was wounded. He called for volunteers to go out with him. Carroll and Straub had succeeded in reaching the trench, the latter shot through the thigh. Carroll at once volunteered for a second trip. Corporal Finucane, Corporal Richard Foy, and Private John Duffy said they would go.[9] Carroll later told me that he was lying with Duffy in the trench when Hayes came and said that the captain was wounded out in front and that he wanted four men to go out with him. Duffy jumped up and said: "I'll go. When do you start?"

The party of five left the trench, crawled around the wire and through the grass. Each carried a hand grenade. They did not find me, owing doubtless to the fact that I lay beyond the tramway, and Hayes concluded that the Germans had crawled out and captured me. Then he jumped to his feet with the others and threw their grenades at the shell hole. Hayes told me that four of the five grenades went in. The Germans must have seen the party while they were crawling, for they threw grenades and fired with rifles at the same time. Carroll was hit by a bullet in the side and also by a "potato masher" giving him nine wounds from head to foot. The five then crawled back, even Carroll making the trench. They were assisted by a heavy fire from those left in the trench. If I had raised my head I would have seen what was going on and could doubtless have made my way back with the others.

The day wore on and I made no move. I was thirsty and had a canteen on my belt, but was fearful of moving my arm to get it. I waited there for fifteen hours. About ten o'clock in the evening I rolled over and got my first drink from the canteen. I had decided during the day that the better course would be to crawl along the tramway in the dark and then to jump it at a place not directly in front of the shell-hole. So I took off my belt and gas-mask and began to move along on my elbows and toes. The moon was bright, but there was a shadow along the tramway that was in my favor. After a minute or two of this crawling I heard a slight noise and lifted up my head. Lying up against the bank was a man. By reaching out my arm I could have touched him. Then there were two or three shots just ahead. It was apparent that a party of Germans had crawled out, was using the bank as a breastwork, and firing at our people. I backed off the way I had come, until I returned to where I had left my equipment. I then decided to take the shortest route back. I jumped the track and lay on the south side. Nothing happened. I crawled through the grass toward the river for a distance and then leaped up and ran. I missed Hayes's post and kept on until I tumbled into the railroad track, where a platoon of E Company was assembled. A little later a party from Hayes's trench came in, carrying Straub.[10] Carroll was walking, wrapped up in a blanket. We dressed his wounds in the company dugout and sent him back to Mont Notre Dame with three or four others who were wounded.

The conduct of Hayes and his party of Irishmen was the bravest piece of work that came within my experience.[11] These five men came out in broad daylight. There was no cover for them. They came after the enemy had already been attacked and when they were sure to be on the alert. They knew what they were in for. Their success in attacking the post was due entirely to their dash and boldness. As for Carroll, it was his second trip that morning. His wounds kept him in the hospital for four months. Finucane was made mess sergeant a few days later. Foy was made sergeant and Duffy corporal. All five as well as Straub and myself, were awarded the Distinguished Service Cross, the award to Hayes being after his death.[12]

During the night we collected a ration party and sent it back to the kitchen. The enemy was "gassing" Mont Notre Dame that night. The result was that the ration detail was gassed, as were all the cooks and the man guarding our packs. So no rations came up.

VII

I wrote a short account of what had happened, along with a sketch of the German positions as I had found them, and sent the message back to Major Thacher. The runner came back with the news that he had located the place where battalion headquarters had been, but that there was no one there. I sent out another runner, with the same result; I then waited until daylight, when I started out myself, taking Private George La Fleur with me. We searched around, then crossed the river and walked toward Mont Notre Dame. We smelled gas and put on our masks for a time. My mask had been left out in front and I had only a little French mask that one of the men had found for me out in the fields. The gas came through it, so I took it off. I thought that the gas was not strong enough to do any harm.[13]

Near Mont Notre Dame we found a soldier who led us to battalion headquarters. It seems that headquarters had been moved back across the river, and that a man who had been left at the former place to give information of the change had gone off somewhere to sleep. We had breakfast there, I delivered my message, and we went back across the river. We both went to sleep in the little dugout.

I awoke about noon and found my eyes smarting. There seemed to be a brown haze over everything. La Fleur could not see at all. Lieutenant Joseph F. Byrne came up for duty with the company, bringing some cans of salmon that were most welcome. Byrne was killed that night as he stood on the railroad tracks.[14]

We expected a relief that night, August 15th, from K Company. (As it turned out, K Company did not come up until the night of the 16th, which made it necessary for the company to stay in the front for another day.) I arranged with Hayes that I would go back to Mont Notre Dame to get first-aid for my eyes and that I would join the company there as it marched through. Private George Madden accompanied me back to the first-aid post. There the doctors put a bandage on my eyes and put me in an ambulance bound for the field hospital. I was barely conscious. After considerable bumping about, the ambulance reached a field hospital near Fere-en-Tardenois, where I stayed for six days.[15]

The first two days I could not see. I was in a tent with several other officers, all on stretchers. I recall that Captain Roger Lapham was one of these officers.[16] After I recovered my sight my eyes were bloodshot for some weeks. The gas affected my throat also, giving me a cough that lasted for months. But I felt strong and fit in general, and had a great curiosity as to what the company was doing. It was August 22nd when I returned to the company.

VIII

I found F Company in a large wood about two miles south of the Vesle. The position was in support. The kitchen was nearby and the rations came up regularly. Large details of men were at work digging trenches to serve as a support position in case of an enemy offensive. The other companies of the battalion were at hand, and the time passed pleasantly. I learned that all our baggage had been lost in Mont Notre Dame, due to the fact that the guard had been gassed. A French company had looted it, taking every razor they could find. Everything I possessed was gone. For a month or more the entire company had to rely on the razors that ten or fifteen men had kept in their pockets. At this place we lost Archie Van Patten, a company runner,

Robert Patterson, center-right second row, with bandage below nose, triage hospital station in La Chalade, France, mid-August 1917. Standing in foreground at left, Lt. Charles DeWolf Gibson of Company K, 306th Infantry. To the right of Gibson, with a large bandage under his nose, is Robert Patterson, then suffering from the effects of phosphene gas. From collection of the Patterson family.

and Wallace Searles, one of the men around the kitchen. Both were killed by shell-fire.

IX

On the night of August 25th the 2nd battalion went up to the front. The dispositions had been changed. G Company went to the railroad tracks north of the river, where E and F had been. E Company, now under Captain Charles Johnstone, was directly behind on the south bank. H Company was in St. Thibault, a little village on the south side opposite Bazoches. F Company was split into two pieces. The 1st and 2nd platoons were posted on a steep wooded hill a half mile southwest of St. Thibaut; the 3rd and 4th platoons were on the side of a hill fully a mile to the east, with a broad valley between. I was with the 1st and 2nd, but each night I would make the trip over to the other platoons. Cecil Russell, one of the company runners, would act as guide. He was the best man I have ever known for finding his way in the dark. All of the men dug funk-holes and made themselves comfortable.

The second night the Germans put down a great many gas shells on the 3rd and 4th platoons. We had to evacuate about fifteen men the next morning, among them Corporal Thomas Laino who was so far gone that he died a day or two later.

The news got around that G Company was to attack Bazoches on the 27th. They were to be assisted by machine gunners and by an extra platoon. I was called on to furnish the extra platoon and chose my 1st platoon because it had not been at the front on the previous session. The platoon moved off in the dark. Except for three men who came back wounded early in the fight, we saw none of them again until after the armistice. I recall that Robert Daescher and Giuseppe Fiero were two of these men; the name of the third I have forgotten.

The attack was made before dawn from the position on the tracks west of the town. The company went forward in fine style over the field in front, broke through the German lines there, wheeled around to the right and

Saint Thibault Church. From Adler, *History of the Seventy-seventh Division.*

The Vesle Sector

entered the town at the north end. Two platoons of G Company, along with the machine gunners and the platoon from F Company, then advanced further north and dug in. The other two platoons of G Company swept down through the town and dug in at the south end near the railroad station. Bazoches was found to be full of Germans, and the two platoons that went through it had their hands full. They lost heavily in the street fighting. Seventy Germans were captured, however, and at first all went well. The enemy immediately counter-attacked from the east and west and recovered part of the town. It soon developed that the platoons in the rear were too far behind those up forward. This was not the fault of Captain Bull, as he had explicit and detailed orders as to where each platoon should be established. Contact between the two bodies was lost. By noon the two platoons in the rear were so shattered that a retreat was imperative. Bull and eight men from one platoon, with the surgeon, succeeded in swimming the Vesle and getting to safety on the south side. Lieutenant Gordon Gregory and four men from the other platoon did the same thing. The force forward had been surrounded by this time. It held out until well into the afternoon when it was obliged to surrender. Practically all the German prisoners were retaken. Our casualties in this affair were heavy. Twenty-two men of our 1st platoon were captured. Halter was so badly wounded that he died in a German hos-

Major Charles W. Whittlesey, left. From National Archives.

pital. Corporal Albert Lewis and Ed Duffy were also badly wounded and were picked up by the Germans. About eighty men of G Company were also captured. Many others of G Company were killed in the street fighting. Lieutenant Daniel O'Neale of that company died of wounds received in this action. Lieutenant Loren F. Collins was wounded. Lieutenant Jonathan Reid had been wounded the night before. Lieutenant Horace Stokes and a machine gun lieutenant were captured. G Company had only twenty men after the fight and was wholly ineffective until it was filled up with replacements a month later.[17] The incident confirmed me in the opinion that small local attacks by one or two companies were useless and expensive operations. The enemy was able to concentrate their forces on the spot in question and to bring the offensive to a halt.[18] The situation in respect to major offensives was of course quite different.

X

On the night of the 28th we were relieved by the 1st battalion, C Company relieving F. We marched back to a reserve position near Sergy and bivouacked in a small patch of woods along the Ourcq River. Here we remained for a week. The division established a school for combat work here. I attended the school for three or four days. It was here that I became acquainted with Captain Charles Whittlesey of the 308th Infantry, who as leader of the "Lost Battalion" was to become one of the popular heroes of the war.[19] I was told by Lieutenant Theodore Kenyon of B Company that I could get a pair of breeches at the field hospital near Fere. The idea appealed to me, as the only breeches I possessed were out both at the knees and at the seat. So Kenyon and I walked over one evening and I procured without cost an excellent pair of Bedford cord breeches. Upon my return to the company we received a message to be prepared to move out. We made ready and marched into Sergy but waited there for the rest of the night and most of the morning.

The Aisne

It was September 4th when we moved up from reserve. The Germans had just withdrawn from the Vesle and were dug in along the Aisne, a much larger river five or six miles north of the Vesle. Our 1st battalion followed them.[1] It was in a local attack along the Aisne at this time that my old friend Jim Cleveland was wounded and Pat O'Brien of C Company was killed. Cleveland was then in command of A Company, though still a 2nd lieutenant. He was hit by three bullets in the arm and one in the chest and was thereafter out of the war. He was hit while capturing a small patch of woods called La Cendrière. The lines remained on the Aisne practically without change until we left the sector on September 15th.[2]

We marched up and spent a night at our old place on the hill behind St. Thibault. The next day we crossed the Vesle into Bazoches. The village was thoroughly wrecked from the August fighting.[3] I walked out to the place where I had been on the patrol on August 14th and found my rifle and other equipment.[4] We went forward about a mile and spent the night on the side of a hill north of Bazoches. Everything was quiet here.

The next day the captains went forward to look over the positions to be taken. We stopped at Vauxcéré where regimental headquarters had been opened. Ellsworth then took us up the valley and over the plateau between the Aisne and the Vesle. We were to be in support position some distance behind the Aisne, H Company on the right, F Company on the left, and E Company behind. We went back and after dark brought up the companies.

The position of F Company here was in a ravine, with trenches on the open ground nearby. We were the left company of the division and formed a combat liaison group with the French on our left. The 3rd platoon under Sergeant Johnson was in and near a cave with a French company. The 4th platoon under Lt. Richard Blazer was in the ravine, with trenches to the left to be occupied in case of alarm. I stayed in this center position. The 2nd platoon under Hayes was half a mile to the right. They were also in the edge of the ravine, with trenches just behind them. A day or two later a platoon of E Company was sent up to us, to give us four platoons, and these men I kept with the 4th platoon in the center.

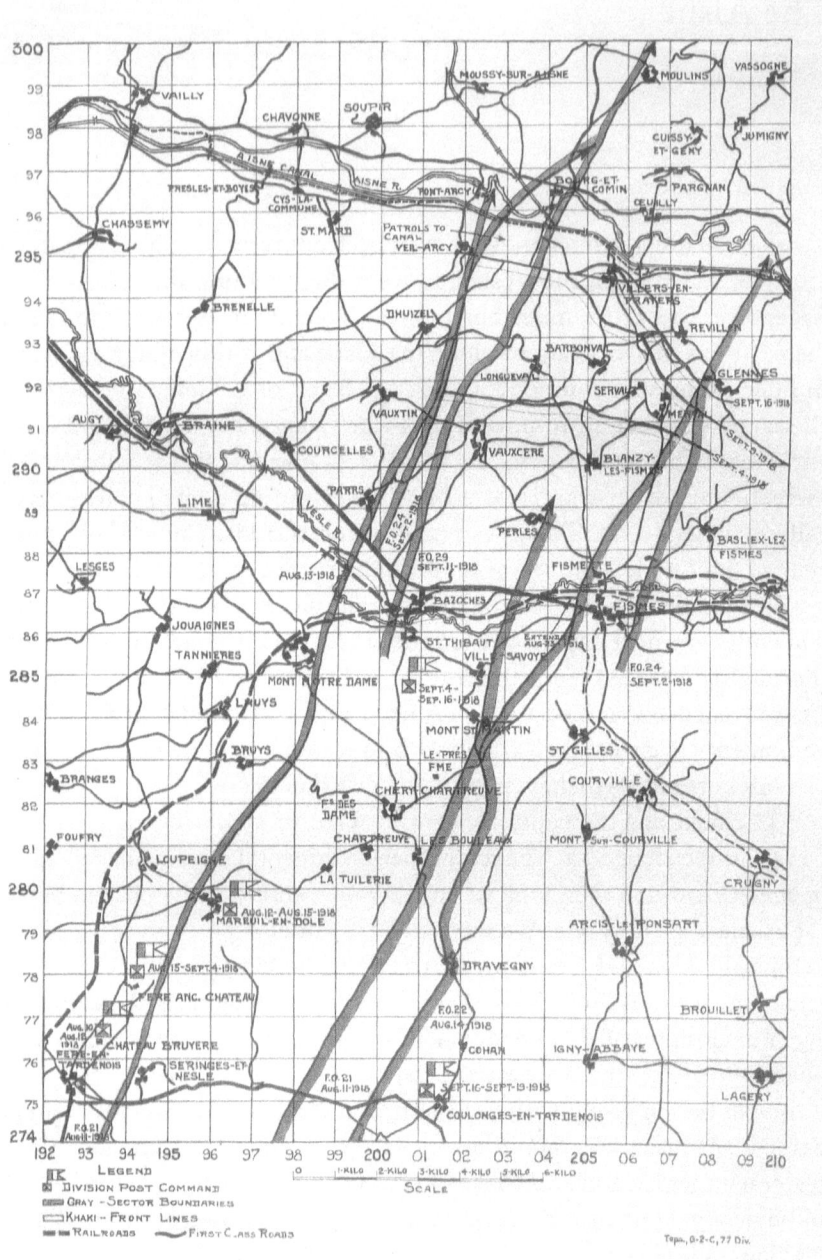

Map 5. 77th Division movements in the Vesle-Aisne Sector, August 11 to September 18, 1918. From Adler, *History of the Seventy-seventh Division.*

Services were held in a shell-torn church. From Adler, *History of the Seventy-seventh Division.*

The place was a quiet one. We had almost no casualties. The only bad features were the rainy weather and the difficulty over rations. As the kitchen was back at Vauxcéré, the carry for a ration party was a long one. The second night the ration detail got lost, wandered around the plateau all night, and came back without anything. We fell back on our reserve rations. The next night I conducted the ration detail myself and very nearly got lost in the rain and dark. Even then the rations were cold long before we could bring them up. Meanwhile the French who were with us were receiving excellent rations. This was due to their use of a light cart drawn by one horse. By such means they could bring their food hot up to the support positions. Our kitchens were heavy things drawn by four horses and were such large targets that they had to be left far in the rear.

We stayed four days in this position. As we were about to take over the front line along the river, we were relieved by an Italian division.[5] We marched back in the dark, without a halt until we had crossed the Vesle. We then went to Ville Savoye and rested two days. From there we marched two nights toward the rear in the regular fashion, fifty minutes of marching and ten minutes of resting. During the days we rested in woods. Trucks then picked us up near Vezilly on the 16th, took us through Chalons and turned up north again. We got off at a little village called Givry, where we remained a day or two. We now learned that our destination was the Argonne and that a big offensive was in prospect. Two more night marches brought us up through Les Islettes to La Chalade, a little town in the depth of the forest. The front line was a mile or so beyond.

The Argonne

I

The Argonne is a large forest, with thick underbrush that makes walking very slow. It has deep ravines running generally east and west.[1] One could find his way through only by relying on the compass. We were in the offensive from its commencement on September 26th until October 15th.

The front on which the attack was launched ran from the Meuse to the western edge of the Argonne. The movement that was commenced on September 26th was called the First Argonne-Meuse Offensive. There were six or seven divisions in the front, with others in reserve. The 77th Division was the left division in the attack. Its front was across the forest and proved to be so wide that eventually every infantry soldier was put into line. After the first two or three days we had no battalions in support. This led to trouble.[2]

II

We stayed in the vicinity of La Chalade for four days, in readiness to attack. The 305th Infantry was also there, and I saw Charles de Rham of that regiment, who was killed at the opening of the attack a few days later. We had good quarters in French trenches there and had very little to do. The French troops remained in the front trenches in order to conceal the presence of Americans in the sector.[3]

On the 25th a large number of replacements came up. F Company received one hundred and ten of them. Our losses on the Vesle had reduced us to about seventy men for duty in the platoons. We had more on the rolls, but quite a number were serving as runners and cooks, and on special detail with the supply company. I now reconstituted the 1st platoon, putting Sergeant Faucher in command and giving him Zimmerman as extra sergeant and William Murphy, John Duffy, Joseph Scott, and Frank Carney for corporals. Practically all the privates in the platoon were replacements. Sergeant Joseph Lo Bono was transferred to G Company which received two hundred of the new men. Lieutenant Blazer was detached for duty with

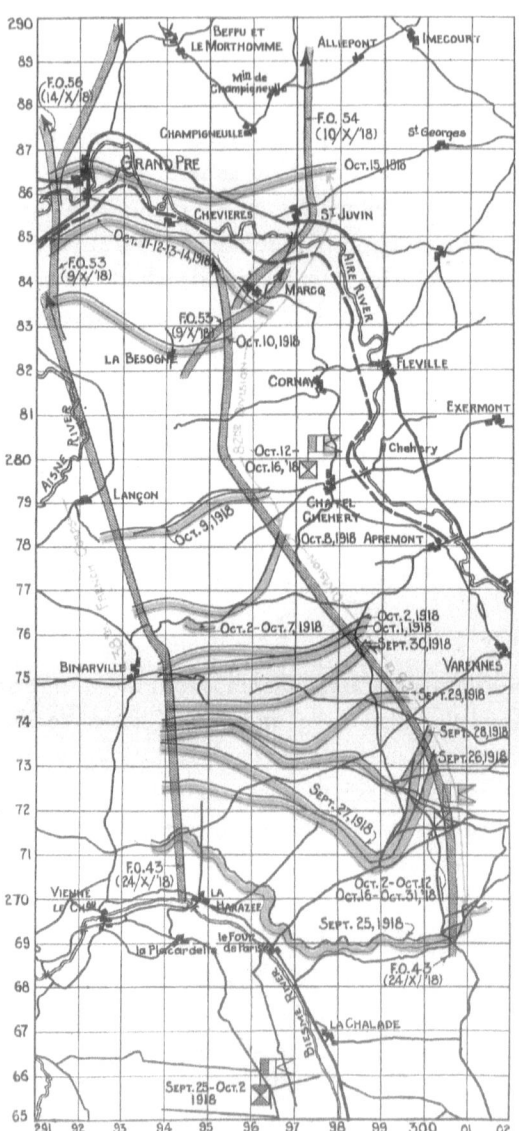

Map 6. The 77th Division in the first phase of the Meuse-Argonne Offensive, September 28 to October 18, 1914. From Adler, *History of the Seventy-seventh Division*.

Spirit of the Argonne. From Adler, *History of the Seventy-seventh Division.*

H Company and remained there until the middle of October. Sergeant Frederick Peterson took charge of the 4th platoon. He was a brave soldier who knew his business thoroughly. Hayes and I were now the only officers in F Company.

These new fellows came from the Northwest. They were excellent men but very green.[4] We gave them hasty instruction on hand grenades, rifle grenades, and gas. In the fighting that followed, they behaved well. There is no doubt, however, that their inexperience was the cause of losses that might have been avoided. A seasoned soldier, on halting at a place near the front, gets his pick or shovel out and begins to dig a funk-hole at once, thereby protecting himself to a considerable extent. A raw man does not realize the value of such cover and is slower about digging. One feature of the fields where fighting had occurred was the long lines of funk-holes that could be seen stretching across the country. Another feature of course was the equipment that had been abandoned.

One of the new men, Reuben Pierson, I made a sergeant during the fight at St. Juvin, and another, a very young fellow named Clayton Nichols, I made a corporal. Among these men there was an Indian, Andrew Washington, who proved to be skillful at scouting and patrolling.

General Robert Alexander, who in August had succeeded General George B. Duncan in command of the division, made a speech to the officers of our brigade, explaining the objects of the coming offensive.[5] I recall with pleasure that after the speech General Edmund Wittenmyer, our brigade commander, introduced me to General Alexander and was kind enough to tell him that I was one of his best fighting captains, adding a few words about my action near Bazoches.

III

The artillery began the offensive at two in the morning.[6] The infantry attack came at six in the morning of the 26th.[7] In our regiment the 1st battalion led off, followed by the 3rd in support. The 2nd was held in reserve at La Florent. The news that came back from the front was good. The 1st battalion had followed the barrage and had advanced more than a mile, capturing a number of prisoners. We were moved up to a place on the road above the fork called Le Four de Paris and spent the night of the 26th there. It was raining hard and everyone was thoroughly soaked.[8] In the morning I saw a little concrete "pill-box" beside the road. Bull and Lt. Gordon Gregory of G Company were in possession. I managed to get in, and a little later Hayes crawled in. Quarters were cramped, but it was a relief to find a dry place.

General Robert Alexander, who commanded the 77th Division during the battles of 1918. From Julius Adler, *History of the Seventy-seventh Division*.

In the afternoon the companies went into German huts and dugouts a little south of the road. Hayes and I had a hut with a little stove and two beds. We dried out thoroughly. A day or two later we moved two miles further up the road, expecting to be sent to the front at any minute. We passed the night in the woods.

The next day I was ordered to report to General Wittenmyer, a grand old man who commanded our brigade.[9] He told me that there was a gap of nearly a mile between the 305th Infantry and the 28th Division (Pennsylvania National Guard) on the right; that I was to fill up this gap with my company; and that I was to report to and take orders directly from him. Late in the afternoon we moved forward on the road, with scouts well ahead, until we heard shooting close at hand. I then halted the company and with two men went over to the right to find the left flank of the 28th. We stumbled around in the dark but finally located the Pennsylvania people. Their line came almost up to the road. F Company was then deployed from this place over to the left. It was dark, the woods were very thick, and we could not find the right flank of the 305th.[10] We stretched the line out as far as we could and waited for daylight. In the morning we located the right battalion of the 305th, commanded by Major Duncan Harris. I then adjusted our line so as to cover the entire gap. About noon Finucane brought up the kitchen and we had a hot meal.[11] There was considerable firing at this place, several men being wounded. Corporal Thomas Murphy, who had come over with me from Headquarters Company, was hit in the leg. The wound did not appear to be a bad one, but it was a day before he could be evacuated. He lost his leg.[12] One of the troubles in the Argonne was the scarcity of roads. What roads were there were filled with trucks bringing rations and ammunition, and it was hard to get ambulances up.[13] In the early part of October there were times when the wounded had to wait over twenty-four hours before ambulances could take them back.[14]

IV

On October 4th the company was recalled from the position on the right flank. We joined the rest of the battalion and relieved the 2nd battalion of the 305th in a part of the forest known as the Bois de la Naza.[15] The 305th

Major General Robert Alexander in the office dugout in the Argonne Forest. From National Archives.

General Alexander's dugout headquarters from the outside. Sign reads "Chief of Staff." From National Archives.

had that day made an attack and had been repulsed with heavy losses. We found the line on the edge of a plateau, with a deep ravine just behind. Two platoons went into funk-holes in front; the other two were on the reverse slope of the hill behind. Patrols reported that the German machine gun posts were only thirty yards in front, but they were rendered invisible by the brush which was very thick at this place. The fire from the machine guns was heavy. Hayes organized a group of men with rifle grenades and threw over showers of these weapons. We also threw phosphorous grenades which were issued to us here for the first time. These grenades had a long stick that was inserted in the barrel of a rifle. On being shot into the air they burst into flame. H Company was on our right, G on our left, and E in the rear.

It was at this place that Corporal Cyrus Patterson of H Company was killed. In H Company there were two Pattersons, Sergeant Dan and Corporal Cyrus. Both of them were fine soldiers. Dan Patterson and I were on very good terms. The other Patterson, Cyrus, crawled out through the bushes on a patrol of his own. He returned a little later and cut two notches in the butt of his rifle for two Germans he had shot in a machine gun nest in the bushes in front. Then he went out again, saying that it was easy and he was going to get some more. He never returned. A day or two later his body was found, shot in several places. It had not been so easy the second time.

On October 7th we advanced in open order across the plateau and met with little resistance as the Germans were withdrawing.[16] The advance was by the compass, North 30 degrees West. As we went forward, I could see only two or three men on each side, and found myself wondering whether all were coming along. Then we crossed a little path, and I could see the troops crossing it far up and down. The thought then came to me of how reliable

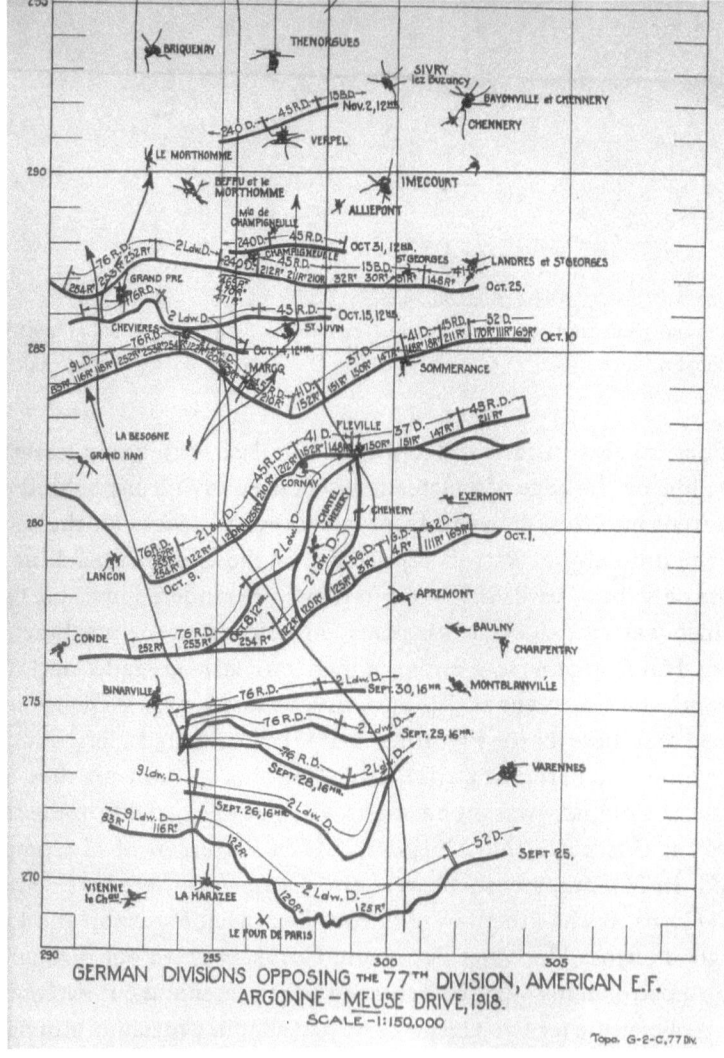

Map 7. German Divisions Opposing the 77th Division, American E.F. Argonne—Meuse Drive, 1918. From Adler, *History of the Seventy-seventh Division.*

the soldiers were. I was the only officer in the company that day, and the men were under the direct immediate orders of no one. Not even a corporal could see all his men. They all went because they knew that it was expected of them. (We had three men in F Company who usually managed to slip out when the company was on the way to the front. Reliefs were generally made in the dark and a man could disappear without much trouble. These fellows would claim to have been lost and would work for an artillery or engineer outfit until we came back again. Except for these three, the soldiers all performed their duties faithfully and cheerfully.)[17]

We halted for the night, a rainy one, beside the Charlevaux road running east and west across the forest. There was no enemy immediately in our front. Hayes had been in the rear that day to bring up new officers to the battalion. Lieutenant Church joined F Company. He was from Torrington, Connecticut, and proved to be a valuable officer.

The place where we passed the night was a little east of the position that had been held by the "Lost Battalion" from October 2nd to 7th. We had not heard of this event, although we were never more than two miles distant. A battalion of the 308th under Whittlesey had broken through the German lines and had pushed forward through the woods to the Charlevaux road, which was the objective they had been ordered to reach. As no other troops had succeeded in breaking through and as there were no men in support of them, Whittlesey's battalion was isolated. The enemy sensed the situation

Cher Ami, the carrier pigeon released by Major Whittlesey on October 4, 1918, with a message that saved the Lost Battalion. From National Archives.

and surrounded these companies, at the same time reoccupying the position which Whittlesey had penetrated. The battalion beat off all attacks and held out for five days. They were then rescued, with a loss of more than two-thirds of their strength.

The next two days were spent advancing through the forest without opposition. The drive of the 1st Division east of the Argonne had made the Germans anxious about their forces in the forest and they were withdrawing.

The "pocket" where some five hundred men from two battalions of the 308th Regiment, 77th Division, fought off attacking German forces for five days, October 2–7, 1918. From National Archives.

On October 10th we came to fields near Grand Ham, the first open country we had seen since September 21st. The company advanced up a road in the woods to a point about a mile south of Grandpré and there halted for a time.

The Aire river runs along the northern border of the Argonne. On the north bank is Grandpré, with St. Juvin about three miles to the east. On the south side are two small places, Chevières and Marcq. The German line was on the north bank.

Major Thacher, Captain Turnbull of a machine gun company, and I went forward to reconnoiter. We passed a chateau that was in flames (la Noue le Coq) and stood on a hill overlooking Grandpré. We must have been seen, because as we were returning a "whiz-bang" (a shell from a 77 millimeter gun) passed waist high between Turnbull and me and exploded four feet beyond us. It was a close call.[18]

F Company was ordered to take a position behind Chevières, with one platoon in the town. Faucher took the 1st platoon in and established posts along the river. The town was burning, making a bright light in the dark. I took the other three platoons to positions in the ditch beside the road in the rear. The night passed without incident, except that a gas attack made us move up the hill a short distance. There were no casualties. During the night I took a captain of engineers up to Cheviéres to see what the chances were of laying a bridge. We found Faucher's men well posted.

The next day, the 11th, we were relieved by the 307th Infantry. We retired into the forest two miles and had a two days' rest, near a little village known as La Besogne.

V

On the night of the 13th we moved through the woods to the east. An attack was to be made on St. Juvin, the 1st battalion to lead and the 2nd and 3rd to follow. About 5 a.m. I was told by Major Thacher to take F Company up to form part of the 1st battalion in the attack. It seemed that B Company was very weak in numbers and would be used only for liaison work. So we went forward to the edge of the woods, where Major Weaver, commanding the 1st battalion, posted us on the right in support of D Company (Captain Henry W. Lehmkuhl). The objective was St. Juvin across the river.

We jumped off at eight thirty and moved down the open fields between the forest and the river. I led the left, Hayes the right. We passed through heavy shelling. It seemed as if we could not get through alive.[19] As a matter of fact, only a few men were hit, the company having been well spread out and having kept their intervals steadily. We stopped in a little sand quarry to reorganize. Here we had some casualties from a shell that landed in the quarry. Corporal James O'Donnell, Pvt. Matthew Lanfear, Jacob Drabkin, and several of the new men were wounded.[20] There had been a sad incident in the field just before. One of two brothers in the company named Ulness had been killed in the sight of the other brother.[21]

The quarry was on a little hill. Down in front was a railroad track, then the river, then a wide field and then St. Juvin on a hill. D Company went down the hill, under machine gun fire from St. Juvin. I prepared to follow. It was arranged that I would go down and find a position on the track, from which we could find fords and cross the river. Upon my signal Hayes was to send the men down from the quarry in small groups.

I ran down the hill and was talking to Lehmkuhl when I heard bursts of fire from the town. I turned around and saw Hayes running down the hill. He made a target, with his light trench-coat and a stick in his hand—obviously an officer. The bullets were clipping around him. Suddenly, when he was most of the way down, he went down. Lehmkuhl and I ran out to him, followed by a man with a stretcher. Hayes had been shot just above the left ear, the bullet passing through his head. We carried him in beside the track and put a bandage on his head. He was unconscious. I held him propped up for two or three hours, still living but never regaining consciousness. Then I had four big fellows take him on a stretcher back to the first-aid station near Marcq. He died on the way back.[22]

I have already given an account of the character of Hayes. I will say again that a better soldier never lived. His purity of character, his devotion to the cause he was fighting for, his instinctive kindness, his courage—these made him a marked man. His body now rests in Arlington Cemetery at Washington.

VI

The town was captured in the afternoon by H Company which had crossed the river over to the east and had then attacked from that side. Over three hundred prisoners were captured.[23] H Company moved forward to a hill north of the village.[24] I had no information of these things at the time. All that I knew was that the companies of the 1st battalion that were near me had crossed the river while I was attending to Hayes. Lieutenants John L. Sweeney of A Company, Gordon Gregory of G Company, Matthew Harkins of E Company and Elverton Crandall of Headquarters Company had also been killed in this attack, and the loss of our regiment in soldiers had been large.

I sent out Sergeant Philip Shedlin of the 2nd platoon with a party to find fords in the river, but it was now dark. I then sent Sergeant Charles Johnson and a party of the 3rd platoon across the river for information. They returned to tell me that the town was empty. On a second trip to find battalion headquarters, a large shell caught the party while crossing the Aire. Johnson and Yaeger were killed and eight others were wounded. Johnson had been one of the mainstays of the company, a brave, dependable man. He had been a fireman in the New York City Fire Department before the war. There is a tablet in his memory in a fire station on the West Side. The same shell wounded Sergeant Breitwieser. The 3rd platoon was thereafter in charge of Sergeant Hugo Fantin.

At this point I should mention Corporal John Miller of the 3rd platoon. He was one of those wounded. The men came back to the railroad track and I passed along the line of wounded lying there. Miller said that his case could wait until others were given first aid. When we finally came to him we found him hit in the face, with his eye down on his cheek. I am happy to say that he did not lose the sight of this eye.[25] He was a quiet, patient man who always did his duty faithfully, a student for the ministry before the war.[26]

VII

By this time I was satisfied that the regiment had advanced. I decided to move the company forward without further delay. A ford was found over to the right where the water was waist-deep. We went over just before dawn, crossed a large low field and found many companies on the side of a steep hill to the east of St. Juvin, just north of the highway running from St. Juvin to Fléville. The 4th platoon was in the lead with me and also reached this hill. The other platoons were still in the low field near the river when a heavy barrage came. It was the worst that I saw in the war.[27]

The hill was so steep that the men on the reverse slope were relatively safe. But the field below seemed to rise and fall. The shells peppered it from the hill to the river. The bombardment continued for an hour. I thought the three platoons down there were done for. After the shooting was finished the men came in, and to my astonishment not one had been hit. The field was very soft and muddy and as the shells would land they would penetrate two feet or more before exploding. Geysers of mud were thrown up, but the mud choked the metal and prevented fragments from flying far. This fact must account for the safety of the men lying in that field. If it had had a hard surface, many would have been hit.

VIII

I found Major Thacher on the hill and reported. Shortly after the shelling had stopped, I saw a group of men on a little spur to the south of St. Juvin to the left and slightly behind our hill. They were five hundred yards distant. The point that struck me was their long overcoats. I called Major Thacher's attention to them. He put his field-glasses on them and said that they were Germans. He explained that no one had crossed the river to the west of the town, our left flank thus being open, and that the enemy had doubtless come in from that quarter. The position enfiladed our hill, where many companies of our regiment and of the 305th were packed, the men having intermingled to get on the steepest parts during the barrage. I was ordered to dislodge the party on the hill.

My 4th platoon under Peterson was well in hand. I told him what we had to do and that we had to move fast. What followed proved to me the great value of steady fire by an attacking party. We could not see any target, but everyone fired at the hill, rifles and Chauchats both, while small parties ran forward a short distance, then dropped down and fired. A German machine gun on the hill fired only once, killing Mike Rygg, one of the new men. That was our only casualty. When we were two hundred yards off, a dozen or fifteen men on the hill began to run in the direction they had come from. We found on the hill a concrete machine-gun emplacement, with a dead man sprawled over the gun. Our fire had been too close for the Germans to operate the gun. Shortly after we took the hill, Lieutenant James Henry with a platoon of G Company also arrived. We scoured the town, found nothing, and returned to our position on the east.[28]

While this movement was in progress, H Company and L Company which were posted on the hill north of the town repulsed a counter-attack by infantry that was launched just after the barrage. I received orders to take over the front and to assault the town to the north, Champigneulles, G Company to operate on the left. I had assembled the non-commissioned officers and was arranging details with them when notice came that the entire division was to be relieved that night by the 78th Division and that the attack would not take place. About ten o'clock that night the 78th came in. We filed back on the Fléville road. On reaching Fléville we crossed the Aire and passed through Cornay. Toward morning we arrived at the kitchen in the forest where all fell out, had a meal, and went to sleep.

IX

On the 16th we marched back through the forest to a German camp known as Camp Bouzon. It was near Montblainville. We remained here until our return to the front on October 31st.

A new batch of replacements joined up, mostly men from Tennessee and Arkansas. Major Thacher fell ill and was evacuated.[29] I took command of the 2nd battalion and held the job until after the armistice. Lieutenant Richard R. Blazer, who had now returned to us from H Company, took F Company. Captain Adler also fell sick, and Lieutenant Loren Collins was put in command of H Company. G and E were still under Captains Bull and Johnstone.

General Wittenmeyer left the brigade, to take command of the 7th Division. Colonel William B. Smedberg of the 305th was promoted and took the brigade until shortly before the Armistice. General Michael J. Lenihan then took command and held it until the brigade was mustered out.

We marched back to Varennes one day and had a hot bath. Under the system we turned in all our old clothes, took the bath, and then got a new outfit—coat, breeches, shirt, underwear and socks. This was to get us rid of "cooties," which we had had in great numbers since July. The relief was only temporary, as the "cooties" found us again after a few days.[30] Varennes was on the Aire and east of the Argonne; it was the place where Louis the Sixteenth was caught in his attempt to escape from France.

On October 8, 1918, 194 men of the "Lost Battalion" were able to walk out of the pocket. (111-Signal Corps 42757.) From National Archives.

Entertainers from the Y.M.C.A. came up to Bouzon and put on a show.[31] We had not heard any new songs since we had been in France. They gave us "All out of step but Jim," "Smiles," and "Oh, how I hate to get up in the morning." There was loud applause and the songs were repeated until everyone had learned them.[32]

An amusing thing happened to me during the show. The men of G Company, having no dugouts, had pitched shelter-tents to cover them from the rain. I was leaning against a tent and watching the show. I was wearing an "issue" uniform at the time, with nothing to mark my rank. Suddenly someone gave me a hard shove from behind and called me hard names for leaning heavily on his tent. I saw the man's point of view and walked away, trusting that no one who knew me had seen the incident. I was mistaken here, however. After the war was over and we were mustered out, Private Meyer Tepper of F Company sprang the joke on me.

General Alexander came up to deliver a speech to the officers and noncommissioned officers. He told us that the next offensive would be along the whole front from the English Channel to Verdun, that the enemy line was like a door swinging on hinges, that the hinges were in our front, and that we were the men to smash the hinges. All in all, it was a good, fighting speech.[33]

One of the craters on the road to Varennes, as seen by a military artist. From National Archives, no. 37837.

X

The entire regiment marched up to the front on October 31st, for what was known as the Second Argonne-Meuse Offensive. We found it as we had left it on the 15th—St. Juvin held by the 78th Division and Champigneulles in possession of the enemy. The plan was for the 305th to make the attack on November 1st, and then for the 306th to continue it the next day.

We spent the night in the fields behind Marcq. The push on November 1st was to be a big one, and we saw plenty of artillery in position. About midnight the bombardment opened. It was a grand occasion. Flashes of fire came from all quarters. The roar of the guns was continuous. The guns kept at it until six in the morning.

All three battalions waited near Marcq all day on the 1st. Hayes had been buried nearby and I went to see his grave. Johnson's grave was the next one. We could get very little news of the attack, but finally learned that the advance of the 305th had been small. The 80th Division on the right had made good progress, however, and the 2nd Division still further on the right had made a deep dent in the German line. After the 1st the campaign was largely a pursuit of the retreating enemy which continued until the armistice.

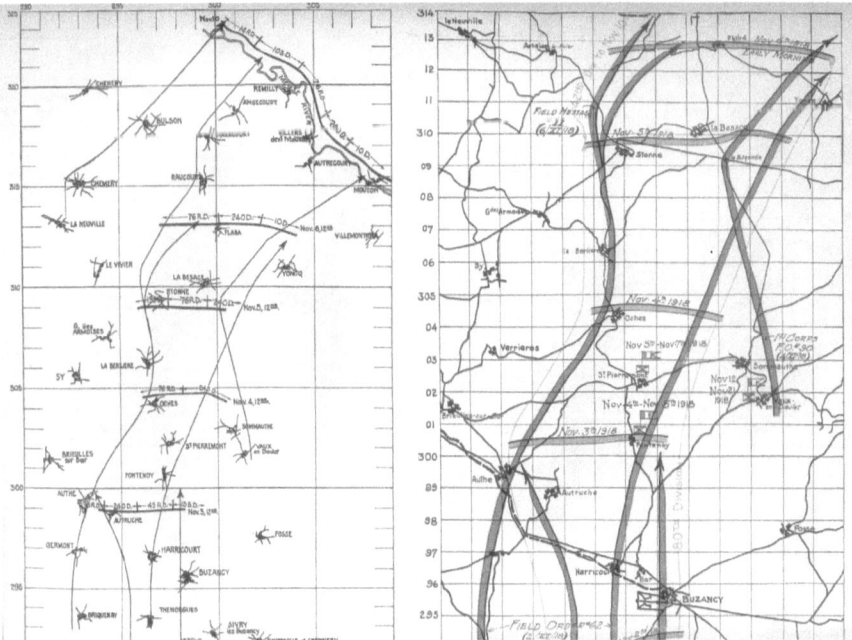

Map 8. The 77th Division in the final Meuse-Argonne Offensive, October 31 to November 6, 1918. From Adler, *History of the Seventy-seventh Division.*

The three battalion commanders (Lehmkuhl of the 1st, myself of the 2nd, John P. Freemen of the 3rd) spent the night at regimental headquarters waiting for orders. Toward morning we received them. The 3rd battalion was to go straight ahead from St. Juvin. The 2nd was to march a mile to the east and then attack toward the northwest. The 1st was to be in support. Outside there was great confusion at the ammunition dump when all three battalions scrambled for cartridges and grenades in the dark at the same time.

We marched across the Aire into St. Juvin. It was then evident that the Germans had withdrawn in the night.[34] I suggested to the regimental commander that the detour I was to make was useless and that I might better push directly on in pursuit along with the 3rd battalion. I was ordered, however, to make the movement as planned. Accordingly we marched out on the road to St. Georges for a mile or more and then took to the fields for Verpel which lay several miles to the northwest. We reached Verpel in the afternoon, long after the 3rd battalion had passed through it. Here I received an order to hold two companies, ready to pursue the enemy on trucks that were coming up. So I remained with F Company and G Company. The other two marched on to Thénorgues.

We spent the night of November 2nd in Verpel. There was plenty of shelling there, but with little damage. Bull, Blazer, and I made a fire in an old house and were comfortable. No trucks appeared.

Varennes, as seen by a military artist. From National Archives, no. 37835.

In the morning I was told that the trucks were not available and to resume the pursuit on foot. We pushed on by the road through Thénorgues, Buzancy, Bar, and Harricourt.[35] These places had already been taken. Above Harricourt we took to the fields headed for St. Pierremont. E and H Companies could be seen far off on the left. German airplanes flew low over us and fired, without effect. Artillery also fired on us, but we encountered no opposition from infantry. Shortly before dark on the 3rd we reached a hill west of St. Pierremont and dug in for the night. On this drive all blankets had been left behind under orders, to make the troops mobile, but the orders were a great mistake. The weather was cold and the men had to tramp up and down all night to keep warm.[36]

We spent November 4th in this position. No rations had come up. We depended on reserve rations and red cabbages that were growing in a field south of the town.

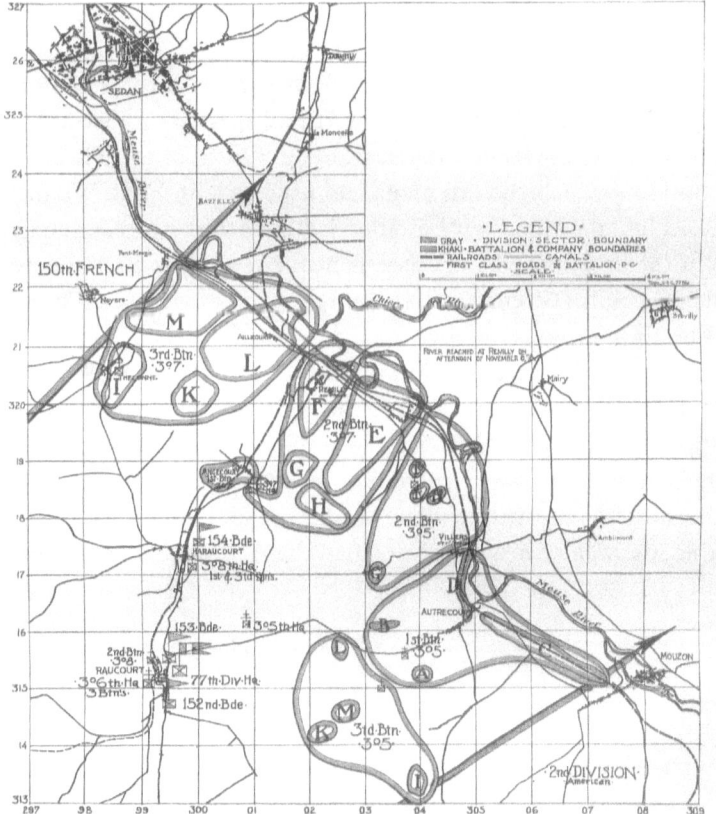

Map 9. The Final Days—November 6–11, 1918. Julius Adler, *History of the Seventy-seventh Division*.

The Argonne

On the 5th the battalion moved forward through St. Pierremont and a large forest north of it, in rear of the 1st battalion. Late in the afternoon we came under shelling in the woods. Carter and a man from the Headquarters Company who was carrying my blanket and rations were killed.[37] The night was a dreary one. A heavy rain was falling and it was cold. The funk-holes dug by the men filled up with water. I was in a wrecked farmhouse with twenty or thirty men. In the farmhouse we made a fire and managed quite well.

There was very little fighting for us in this last offensive.[38] There was a great deal of marching, the distances covered in the daily movements being considerable. We were far in advance of our rations and often went hungry. Another source of trouble was the cold and wet weather which in the absence of blankets deprived the men of the chance of rest.

On the 6th we passed through Le Besace, taken the day before by the 3rd battalion. It was full of French civilians, people who had been under the Germans for four years. The fact that the town was inhabited showed how far we had penetrated into the German rear-area. The towns near the lines had all been empty.[39]

We pushed on toward the Meuse River and spent the night in woods, each man digging a funk-hole. On the 7th we again went forward and took a position about a mile from the Meuse, behind Autrecourt. There was a large brick building which the Germans had used as a hospital. We found it full of the 3rd battalion, but our battalion headquarters managed to get a room down in the basement. In the basement room we found a large iron kettle, in which we boiled cabbage with a little canned corned beef. The companies dug holes in the woods nearby.

On the 8th we were ordered to draw back a mile or more, still in the woods. Here the 1st Division passed through us from right to left in an effort to be the first to reach Sedan.[40]

The 9th and 10th were spent by our battalion in reserve at Raucourt. The division was in the line along the Meuse and we were scheduled to relieve the 305th and cross the river when the Armistice came on the 11th.[41]

After the Armistice

I

At eight in the morning of the 11th, we were told that the Armistice would take effect at eleven.¹ The relief was wonderful. Everyone relaxed. There were no demonstrations.² At night camp fires made their appearance, a thing not to be thought of before. French Algerian troops marched through for Sedan, flags flying and bands playing.

On the 12th we set out for the rear. We had reached St. Pierremont, where orders came to march forward again and take up a position north of the Meuse. So we moved up across the river and spent four days at Autreville. We lived in houses and made ourselves comfortable. Many Italians and Russians who had been prisoners and had been used by the Germans for heavy labor came through our lines. Their condition was pitiable, but their troubles were now behind them.

Our division was to spend the winter near Chaumont, in eastern France. We commenced our march back to this area, travelling back over the same ground we had fought over since September 26th. The first night we reached Bar, the next Fléville, and the next Les Islettes.

II

Leaves were given to officers at Les Islettes, the first opportunity of the kind we had had since our arrival in France. I left with Bull. We boarded a train that dropped us in Paris the next morning. It was my first sight of the French capital. We spent a day there and then went to Nice. As we were getting off the train at Nice, I met Willoughby Middleton.³ We had a great reunion. Bull and I spent a week at the Hotel Negresco. We had plenty of money in our pockets, since for months we had not spent anything. There was a trip to Monte Carlo, Mentone, and over the Italian frontier. On our way back we spent another day in Paris. We rejoined the battalion in winter quarters early in December. Major Bennett, who had formerly had E Company, commanded the battalion, and I resumed command of F Company. E, F, and

H were billeted in Sexfontaines. G Company was in Meures two miles away. We remained here until the middle of February 1919 and had a very comfortable time.

Sexfontaines was a typical French village of thirty or forty houses, with a church, a school and one or two little stores. The people were peasants who walked out to work their little farms. For years they never left the neighborhood. Everything was primitive. The only lights were candles. They had no stoves, only open fireplaces for heating and cooking. They had no water system, not even a pump; all the water was hauled up from wells by hand. Needless to say, there were no automobiles. Yet the people were contented and comfortable.

The day of the soldier was spent in this fashion: there would be reveille formation at seven o'clock; then there would be breakfast and a long morning of drilling in a large field above the village.[4] In the afternoon the men would play cards, loaf about, and so forth. Most of them were billeted in barns that were open to the winds and were very cold in severe weather; yet they thrived on the life and there was practically no sickness.

I was billeted in a little house occupied by an old couple named Ruelle. The old man was quite cheerful and talkative. The old lady was a little queer in the head. Their only son had been killed early in the war, and grief over his loss unsettled her. She would walk around, muttering *"pauvre René, pauvre René."* The house had only two rooms that were used. I had one; the other served as a kitchen, dining-room, living-room, and bedroom for the old people.

III

The company grew in numbers. Many of our original men who had been wounded returned from hospitals, Carroll among them.[5] First Sergeant George West, Corporal Charles Donnelly, Corporal Franklin Williams, and Bugler Marcy Weinberg came to us from Headquarters Company, transferred on their request. Then one day in January fifteen men of the old 1st platoon who had been captured marched in. Sergeant William Hennessy was with them. It seems that he had been captured while on his way back wounded to Mont Notre Dame. A German patrol took him on the south side of the Vesle and brought him to Bazoches. The others had been captured at Bazoches on August 27th. They were bitter over their treatment as prisoners. Corporal Lewis told me of their experiences.[6] For a month they were held at Laon, working in the railroad yards. There was very little to eat. Then they were sent to a prison camp at Rastatt, in Baden. Here they received a package every week from the American Red Cross in Switzerland, and the food in it was enough to keep them in good condition without touching the prison rations.

Lewis gave me an interesting account of what Ed Duffy did in Bazoches. He told me that "Big Ed" was a terror, running all over the place, sometimes with two or three others and sometimes alone. He had killed many Germans and was the outstanding hero of the fight. He was fired on from a house and on running into the house was shot through the lower jaw. This did not stop him. He took three prisoners in the house and was marching them up the street when he was shot through the chest from the rear. This brought him down. His prisoners escaped. Duffy crawled under a house but was captured later by the Germans who called to him in English and told him that the Americans had taken the town. Lewis said that Duffy was in the German hospital with him, in very bad shape, and that he had died there. Months later, when we were forming at Washington Square for our final parade up Fifth Avenue, a man in civilian clothes came up and hailed me by name. I recognized him as Ed Duffy, although his chin was a good deal shorter than it had been. He said that he had been very low in the German hospital and one night had been removed to another hospital. The other men in the hospital missed him the next day, but did not know of the removal and concluded that he had died. He had pulled through in the other hospital. After the Armistice he had been sent home as completely disabled. I have seen him once since that time. He appeared to be fairly strong and in good health.

The addition of the wounded, sick, and captured brought the company up to three hundred men, fifty more than full strength.[7]

At Sexfontaines twenty men were permitted to go on two weeks furlough. I took pains to give these furloughs to men who had been with the company all through the fighting—men like Sam Silverstein, Armando Salvini, and Corporal William Ruppertsburg. Silverstein told me he did not like to leave. "I have been with this company every day since we landed in France. I have never had a soft job like guarding baggage or on the supply detail. All the time I have been in my platoon. Now if I go on furlough, it might spoil my record." I assured him that his record was already made and could not be spoiled. I promoted Silverstein to corporal at this time.[8]

Ruppertsburg had been the life of the company. No matter how dismal things were, "Ruppie" was always there with a funny remark or a caper.[9] He also was made a corporal.

IV

On February 14, 1919, we left Sexfontaines for a new billeting area near Angers.[10] We marched to Bricon and then had a trip of two days by railroad. We left the train at Grez-en-Bouerre. F and G Companies were billeted at Gennes, E and H at Ruillé Froids Fonds four miles away.

I stayed here with an old professor and his sister. Their house was half a mile beyond the town. Lieutenant Duff Reid, who commanded G Company while Bull was on special work in Paris, was billeted in an estaminet (small café) at the end of the main street, and this was the place where most of the officers ate and spent their spare time. Reid was an independent fellow who was continually getting into trouble with colonels and generals, and he kept things lively.

We received an order from regimental headquarters that the appearance of the troops was not what it should be and that hereafter the bottoms of all overcoats should be the same distance from the ground. This was a foolish and thoughtless order. On a very tall man the bottom of the overcoat would be over three feet from the ground. This distance on a short man would bring the bottom of the overcoat up around the shoulders. I did what I could to taper off the overcoats but of course did not carry out the order literally. Reid, however, lined G Company up, read the order, found a man six and a half feet high whose overcoat was three feet off the ground, and ordered all the others to walk past the big man. As they passed a chalk mark was made on their coats to show where the bottom of the big man's coat came. Then all the coats were sewed up according to the chalk mark. The result was that the little men in the 4th platoon had the bottoms of their coats up at their arm-pits. The coat consisted only of a collar and a pair of sleeves. They ran about this way for two weeks, everyone making a big joke of the thing, until an officer from regimental headquarters came to Gennes and saw what was going on. Then the coats came down.

The battalion surgeon was Lieutenant Cackley. He was a good, faithful creature, very literal and gullible. He came from Caldwell, Ohio. The lieutenants, Blazer, Morris and Reid, took delight in telling Cackley tall stories, inventing diseases and describing their symptoms to him. One day General Alexander came to Gennes and summoned the officers. He asked many questions about the work of the soldiers, their recreations and so on. Turning to Cackley he said, "Doctor, I want to hear about the health of the soldiers. How many do you have on sick-call in the morning?" Cackley replied, "We don't hold sick-call in the morning, General. We hold it in the afternoon."

In March there was a review of the entire division for General Pershing. The troops were assembled in a large field and Pershing walked up and down each company front. As he was proceeding along the G Company front he noticed that many of the men had wound stripes. He said to Reid, "Lieutenant, have all your men got wound stripes?" Reid said, "No, sir." The general said, "Why not?" Reid answered, "They were not all wounded, sir." Reid was a bold fellow.

General John J. Pershing. From National Archives.

V

Late in March I was promoted to major and took over command of the 2nd battalion from Major Bennett. My name had been sent in for promotion before the armistice, but with the armistice all promotions were suspended. I owed my promotion to Colonel Vidmer and Major Thacher.

I moved to Ruille where the battalion had headquarters. I was billeted in a chateau beyond the village. Comte Jean de Ruille lived there. The family consisted of the old count and wife, their daughter Ghislaine, their son the young count, and his wife and three children. They were most hospitable and kind. The young count and his sister spoke English easily and I had many talks with them.

VI

It was the middle of April, 1919, when we left Ruille and Gennes. The train took us to Brest, where we embarked on the *Mount Vernon*. The entire 306th was on this ship. There was also a batch of convalescents from a hospital, none of whom had been wounded and who were wholly undisciplined and unruly. General Alexander and the division staff were also on board.

We landed at Hoboken early in May. The first stop was at Camp Mills near Garden City. From there we went back to Camp Upton once more, where on May 9, 1919, the regiment was mustered out. I went to Glens Falls to see my father and mother.

Infantry Equipment and Tactics

I

The rifle of the Regular Army and of the National Guard was the Springfield. I was familiar with this weapon through my experience in Texas. Our regiment as part of the National Army was given the Enfield rifle, a new gun that could be manufactured faster than the Springfield. Like the Springfield, it had a magazine holding five cartridges. While a serviceable rifle, it was not as good as the Springfield; it was not as accurate and it did not have as good a "feel." Soon after we got into serious fighting, most of the men managed to get Springfields.[1] The places where fighting took place were always strewn with equipment of all sorts—rifles, canteens, packs, gas-masks, helmets,

The superior Browning automatic rifle did not reach doughboys until the last weeks of the fighting. (111-Signal Corps 32360.) From National Archives.

grenades and so on—that had belonged to the dead and wounded, and it was easy to pick up Springfields. On the Vesle there were many of these rifles that had been abandoned by the 4th Division which had fought there a few days before we came in.

II

One man in each squad had a Chauchat gun. This was a French weapon, a light machine gun weighing eighteen pounds. The magazine held from sixteen to eighteen cartridges and was semi-circular, like half a pie plate. Two other men in the squad carried, in addition to ordinary rifles, bags of extra magazines for the Chauchat. The gun was a crude affair, with a kind of nozzle at the end, and it was not accurate. But it was fairly effective. The fact is that we rarely saw a clear target to shoot at, and the Chauchat by peppering the landscape generally might do as good work as a gun with greater precision. The disadvantage of the Chauchat was that it took bullets of larger caliber than the ordinary rifle ammunition. It was therefore a job to get rifle ammunition and also Chauchat ammunition.

III

In each squad there was one man with rifle grenades. These also were French. This man carried a *tromblon,* a cup-shaped iron piece that could be fastened on the muzzle of a rifle. The rifle grenade was a cylindrical affair with a hole down the middle. It was placed in the *tromblon,* with the butt of the rifle resting on the ground and the rifle elevated about forty degrees. On firing an ordinary cartridge in the rifle, the bullet passed through the hole in the grenade, hitting a spring and starting the detonation mechanism. At the same time the force of the explosion in the rifle lifted the grenade into the air. The range of this grenade was about one hundred and fifty yards. If properly fired it would explode just before or after reaching the ground, the iron jacket flying in small pieces. It was a powerful weapon, but for some reason was rarely used by the soldiers. Hayes was one of the few officers who saw the good points of the rifle grenade; when in the lines he constantly kept his men at work firing them.

IV

All the soldiers carried hand grenades, and there were supplies of them in all posts. Those used by us were supplied by the French. There was a light one with a tin cover, called the citron. It was shaped like a lemon and had a

155-mm heavy gun. (111 Signal Corps 6367.) From National Archives.

lever on the side. On pulling out a cotter-pin and throwing, the lever flew off and the grenade started to work. Five seconds later came the explosion.

The other hand grenade was heavier and better. It had a steel jacket, checker-boarded. On top was a cap, held on by pitch. When the cap was removed, there was a pin or screw held up by a spring. The soldier would hit this pin against his shoe or his helmet, thus starting the explosion. He would immediately throw the grenade. These grenades had plenty of power. On exploding the jacket broke up into many flying missiles of steel which were deadly. A man could throw them only from twenty to thirty yards, however. They were superior to the German "potato-masher," a light grenade on the end of a stick. The potato-masher had a longer range and made a powerful explosion, but the metal was not heavy. I have seen men take an explosion of a "potato-masher" at close range and get wounds that were only on the surface.

In addition to the weapons already described, the infantryman of course had his bayonet. G Company used bayonets in the street fighting in Bazoches. I myself never saw a man bayoneted.[2]

Toward the end of the war we also had phosphorous grenades. These were fired from a rifle. They burst into flame on the way down to earth and were a terrible missile. We used them only in the Argonne.

V

The rest of the equipment consisted of helmet, gas-mask, trench knife, canteen, shovel or pick, and the pack.

The pack had half of a shelter tent, poncho, two blankets, two days' reserve rations (canned beef and hardtack), an extra pair of shoes, and extra socks, shirt, and underwear. It made a cruel load when added to the rifle, ammunition, and other equipment. The total weight of all equipment was between sixty and seventy pounds. With such a load a man could only put one foot down just in front of the other, instead of taking a good pace. The result was that on marches a company would do well to make two miles an hour.

I always thought that the pack could have been lightened a great deal. The extra shoes and one of the two blankets could have been dispensed with to advantage. This would have been quite a help, as the shoes were studded with nails and were not only heavy but bulky. As it was, we generally left the packs (except the rations) behind on going into action and got no good from the things that were in them. During the Argonne and the November push we had no packs for weeks. If the packs had been lighter, they could have been carried up and one blanket would have been a great comfort.

VI

I will try to describe the formations of an infantry company. The ordinary close-order drilling was the same as had prevailed in the Regular Army before the war. Its value for discipline and for teaching automatic obedience to commands cannot be overestimated.

The open order or skirmish formation before the war had been for the squad to form in one line, with an interval of one yard between men. The advance would be made by men running forward a short distance while the others in the squad lay on the ground and kept up the firing. In training our new men in the United States we had followed this system.

On reaching France we had to teach new formations for attack. For passing through shell-fire in the open fields, we used short squad columns with the corporal in the lead and the men following. The men were spaced quite far apart so as to diminish the chances of many being hit by one shell. On coming under machine gun fire, the officers or sergeants would have these columns formed into lines by the men running up abreast of the corporals. The intervals between the men would be four yards instead of one yard as in the old system. They were supposed to keep going and to shoot at the same time if near enough to do any good.

Usually a company would form for the attack with two platoons in front and two following. When lines were later formed for advancing against machine guns, there would be two waves, one in front made up of the first two platoons and the other some forty yards behind made up of the other two platoons.

It was the job of officers and sergeants to lead the attack, with one or two left to follow in the rear to see that no one stopped or turned back. All officers and sergeants would pay particular attention to keeping the men well spread out as they advanced, whether in column or in line, as the tendency in an attack is always toward a bunching up.[3]

When a man was wounded in the advance, no one was supposed to stop to help him; this job was for the first-aid men and stretcher-bearers who followed in the rear. I might say here that relatively few men were killed outright in the lines. The ratio of the wounded to the killed in the field must have been fully ten to one. If five were killed, there would be fifty wounded. Of course some of those wounded in the lines died later, so that the final ratio would not be as high as ten to one.

I should also point out that while a company could lose a large number of men for a time and be reduced in strength, through wounds, gas, and so on, this would not indicate that many were killed. Quite a number of the wounded and gassed would join up again after a time. In the meantime replacements would have been sent up to fill out the ranks. As I recall it, the number of men killed in F Company was the smallest of any rifle company in our regiment. Among those killed were Lieutenants Hayes and Byrne, Sergeant Johnson, Corporal Laino and Privates Van Patten, Wogatzke, Searles, Jaeger, Carter, Halter, Ulness, and Ryg. I have doubtless forgotten four or five. The wounded were very numerous.[4]

RLs P. Patten

July 10, 1933.

Infantry Equipment and Tactics

Appendix

Official Citations for Robert Patterson and His Men for Receiving the Distinguished Service Cross for Heroism in 1918

Captain Robert P. Patterson.
Near Bazoches, France, August 14, 1918

For extraordinary heroism near Bazoches, France, August 14, 1918. Captain Patterson, accompanied by two non-commissioned officers, made a daring daylight reconnaissance into the enemy lines. He surprised an enemy outpost of superior numbers and personally destroyed the outpost. Later he had an encounter with another outpost, during which several of the enemy were killed or wounded and one member of his patrol wounded. The enemy advanced their outpost, and Captain Patterson covered the retreat of his patrol, during which he dropped into a depression and feigned being killed in order to escape capture. Here he lay until he was able to escape to his lines under cover of darkness. Residence at appointment: Glens Falls, NY.

First Lieutenant Michael Joseph Hayes.
At Bazoches, France, August 14, 1918, and at St. Juvin, France, October 14, 1918

For repeated acts of extraordinary heroism in action at Bazoches, France, August 14, 1918, and St. Juvin, France, October 14, 1918. On August 14 Lieutenant Hayes led a patrol of five men in broad daylight without any cover in an attempt to rescue his company commander, who had fallen wounded near an enemy machine-gun nest. Failing to find the wounded officer, he crawled to within twenty yards of the post, attacked it with great dash and gallantry, inflicting a number of heavy casualties in spite of heavy fire from enemy machine-guns and hand grenades. On October 14 this officer led his platoon forward into the attack with energy and courage, in the face of heavy artillery and machine-gun fire. In the face of direct fire from enemy machine-guns upon his platoon, disregarding his own personal safety, he went forward to reconnoiter and to find cover for his men from which to continue the attack. In the performance of this courageous enterprise he was killed by machine-gun fire. Residence at appointment: 9214 Empire Avenue, Cleveland, Ohio.

Corporal Patrick J. Carroll, Company F.
Near Bazoches, France, August 14, 1918

For extraordinary heroism near Bazoches, France, August 14, 1918. Corporal Carroll led a company of five men to the rescue of his company commander, who was lying concealed within twenty yards of an enemy machine-gun nest. He advanced through the intense machine-gun fire to the enemy's position and, although wounded in nine places, returned to his lines with important information. Residence at enlistment: 158 East 102nd Street, New York, NY.

Corporal Peter Finucane, Company F.
Near Bazoches, France, August 14, 1918

For extraordinary heroism in action near Bazoches, France, August 14, 1918. He voluntarily exposed himself to intense enemy artillery and machine-gun fire, crawling forward, in company with four other men of his company, in search of their wounded company commander, who had fallen a short distance in front of his company's position. After a fruitless search for the wounded officer the patrol engaged the nearest enemy post and in a fight with hand grenades destroyed it. Corporal Finucane then assisted a wounded comrade to return to his own lines. The heroic conduct of Corporal Finucane greatly encouraged the men of his company, inciting them to heroic endeavor. Residence at enlistment: 430 East 137th Street, New York, NY.

Corporal Robert A. Straub, Company F.
Near Bazoches, France, August 14, 1918

For extraordinary heroism in action near Bazoches, France, August 14, 1918. Voluntarily joining a daylight patrol seeking information as to the strength and positions of the enemy which was attacked about one hundred yards beyond its lines by an enemy hostile post of seven men. The enemy was immediately attacked from the rear, several of the men killed and the survivors scattered. A moment later another enemy post was attacked and in hand-to-hand fighting Corporal Straub killed one of the enemy and was himself badly wounded. Although unable to walk and under heavy fire from nearby enemy posts, Corporal Straub dragged himself to his lines and gave valuable information as to the disposition of the enemy forces. Residence at the time of enlistment: 322 East 101st Street, New York, NY.

Private First Class John Duffy, Company F.
At Bazoches, France, August 14, 1918

For extraordinary heroism in action at Bazoches, France, August 14, 1918. Voluntarily joining a daylight patrol seeking information as to the strength and positions of the enemy which was attacked about one hundred yards beyond its lines by an enemy hostile post of seven men. The enemy was immediately attacked from the rear, several of the men killed and the survivors scattered. A moment later another enemy post was attacked and in hand-to-hand fighting Private Duffy killed one of the enemy and was himself badly wounded. Although unable to walk and under heavy fire from nearby enemy posts, Private Duffy dragged himself to his lines and gave valuable information as to the disposition of the enemy forces. Residence at enlistment: 722 Bergen Street, Brooklyn, NY.

Private First Class Richard Foy, Company F.
Near Bazoches, France, August 14, 1918

For extraordinary heroism in action near Bazoches, France, August 14, 1918. He voluntarily exposed himself to intense enemy artillery and machine-gun fire, crawling forward, in company with four other men of his company, in search of their wounded company commander, who had fallen a short distance in front of his company's position. After a fruitless search for the wounded officer the patrol engaged the nearest enemy post and in a fight with hand grenades destroyed it. Private Foy then assisted a wounded comrade to return to his own lines. The heroic conduct of Private Foy greatly encouraged the men of his company, inciting them to heroic endeavor. Residence at enlistment: 495 St. Marks Avenue, Brooklyn, NY.

Notes

Introduction

1. Forrest Davis, "The Toughest Man in Washington," *Saturday Evening Post* (September 5, 1942), 60. "Probably no man in the [Roosevelt] administration was more ruthlessly determined to fulfill his assignment than Patterson." Henry L. Stimson and McGeorge Bundy, *On Active Service in Peace and War* (New York: Harper & Brothers, 1947), 342.

2. It should be noted that Patterson did write formal reports to the Battle Monuments Commission and contributed a detailed critique of Julius Adler's *History of the 306th Infantry Regiment,* http://www.longwood.k12.ny.us/history/upton/adler/adler.htm, in addition to writing his own memoir in 1933.

3. For an excellent annotated bibliography of World War I memoirs, see Edward G. Lengel, *World War I Memories* (Lanham, Md.: Scarecrow Press, 2004). See also Brian Bond, *Survivors of a Kind: Memoirs of the Western Front* (New York: Continuum, 2008).

4. Keith E. Eiler, *Mobilizing America: Robert P. Patterson and the War Effort 1940–1945* (Ithaca, N.Y.: Cornell University Press, 1997), 23.

5. Quoted in Eiler, *Mobilizing America,* 468.

6. J. Garry Clifford and Samuel R. Spencer Jr., *The First Peacetime Draft* (Lawrence: University Press of Kansas, 1986), 121–23.

7. "He had known war at very close range in 1918; he was at war from 1940 onward, and he had a fierce hatred of all delay and any compromise; his only test of any measure was whether it would help to win, and for any group or individual who blinked at sacrifice he had only scorn." Stimson and Bundy, *On Active Service,* 342.

8. See Richard M. Dalfiume, *Desegregation of the Armed Forces* (Columbia: University of Missouri Press, 1969), 150–52.

9. Quoted in Eiler, *Mobilizing America,* 473–74.

10. The most recent historian of the Meuse-Argonne battle asks: "Did all those Doughboys need to die? The dictates of national pride, politics, and diplomacy said yes. America, [General John J.] Pershing and his countrymen believed, had to prove that she could stand alone and powerful on the world stage. Morality—according to some constructions, at least—also dictated that American soldiers must fight and die in the cause of right and justice. The Doughboys themselves never came up with one definitive answer. Some veterans believed they had fought the good fight. Others said it had all been a terrible waste. For most, it was a little of both." Edward G. Lengel, *To Conquer Hell: The Meuse-Argonne, 1918* (New York: Henry Holt, 2008), 420.

11. Quoted in Peter J. Schifferle, *America's School for War: Fort Leavenworth, Officer Education, and Victory in World War II* (Lawrence: University Press of Kansas, 2010), 16.

12. Wardlaw Miles quoted in Richard Slotkin, *Lost Battalions: The Great War and the Crisis of American Nationality* (New York: Henry Holt, 2005), 497.

13. Quoted in Thomas G. Paterson and others, *American Foreign Relations: A History, Volume 2: Since 1895,* 7th ed. (Boston: Wadsworth/Cengage, 2010), 134.

14. Quoted in Michael Pearlman, *To Make Democracy Safe for America: Patricians and Preparedness in the Progressive Era* (Urbana: University of Illinois Press, 1984), 150. A French

soldier described his first encounter with American troops in 1917: "You could not imagine a more extraordinary gathering than this american [sic] army, there is a bit of everything, Greeks, Italians, Turks, Indians, Spanish, also a sizable number of boches. Truthfully, almost half of the officers have German origins. . . . I asked one son of a Frenchmen if these [American] Germans were coming willingly to fight their brothers and cousins, he squarely answered me: 'yes!'" Quoted in Nancy Gentile Ford, *Americans All: Foreign-Born Soldiers in World War I* (College Station: Texas A&M University Press, 2001), 3.

15. Quoted in Clifford and Spencer, *First Peacetime Draft*, 239.

16. Christopher M. Sterba, *Good Americans All: Italian and Jewish Immigrants in the First World War* (New York: Oxford University Press, 2003), 113.

17. Quoted in John W. Chambers, "Conscripting for Colossus," in Peter Karsten, ed., *The Military in America* (New York: Simon & Schuster, 1980), 279.

18. Quoted in Clifford and Spencer, *First Peacetime Draft*, 18.

19. The ethnic diversity of the AEF was striking. Approximately 18 percent of recruits were foreign born, and 70 percent had lived in the United States for less than ten years. Lengel, *To Conquer Hell*, 36.

20. Quoted in Pearlman, *To Make Democracy Safe*, 152.

21. Eiler, *Mobilizing America*, 23.

22. Ibid.

23. Steven Trout, *On the Battlefield of Memory: The First World War and American Remembrance, 1919–1941* (Tuscaloosa: University of Alabama Press, 2010), 2.

Plattsburg

1. Years later, as secretary of war in 1946, Patterson would write: "There can be no democracy in the platoon advancing under fire to take a tactical objective. Only discipline of the highest order can then win the fight and at the least cost in lives. Every soldier knows this—most of all the men who actually carry on the battle." Quoted in Eiler, *Mobilizing America*, 457–58.

2. Paul Fussell famously defined such harassment as "chickenshit"—"behavior that makes military life worse than it need be: petty harassment of the weak by the strong; open scrimmage for power and authority and prestige; sadism thinly disguised as necessary discipline; a constant 'paying off of old scores'; and insistence on the letter rather than the spirit of ordinances. . . . Chickenshit can be recognized instantly because it never has anything to do with winning the war." Paul Fussell, *Wartime* (New York: Oxford University Press, 1989), 80.

3. Patterson's conclusions about discipline are remarkably similar to the chapter entitled "The Meaning of Obedience" in Jennifer D. Keene, *Doughboys, the Great War, and the Remaking of America* (Baltimore: Johns Hopkins University Press, 2001), chap. 3.

4. At the outset of American participation in World War I, there were only 5,791 officers in the regular army. The four-million-man wartime army would eventually require 200,000 officers. At its peak at the end of the war, the army's officers consisted of 4 percent regulars, 6 percent National Guardsmen, and 8 percent commissioned from the ranks, with "ninety day wonders" from the Officers Training Camps comprising 48 percent. The remaining officers were specialists, including doctors, who received direct commissions. Edward M. Coffman, *The Regulars: The American Army, 1898–1941* (Cambridge, Mass.: Harvard University Press, 2004), 205.

5. See John Garry Clifford, *The Citizen Soldiers: The Plattsburg Training Camp Movement, 1913–1920* (Lexington: University Press of Kentucky, 1972).

6. Historian John P. Finnegan has written that Plattsburg "was, in a way, a kind of secular retreat for a generation. There, amid simple martial surroundings, the upper-class elite underwent a conversion experience of patriotism, individual responsibility, and collective action. . . . The army camp had somehow become a paradigm for the good life in America." Finnegan, *Against the Specter of a Dragon: The Campaign for Military Preparedness, 1914–1917* (Westport, Conn.: Greenwood Press, 1974), 66–67.

Camp Upton

1. One of the draftees in the 20th Infantry, 77th Division, was the Broadway composer Irving Berlin, who wrote the morale-boosting musical *Yip, Yip, Yaphank,* with its plaintive ditty, "How I Hate to Get Up in the Morning." Based on Berlin's 1918 musical, the 1943 film *This Is the Army,* starring Ronald Reagan, George Murphy, and Joan Leslie, celebrated the patriotic entertainment performed by the veteran doughboys of Camp Upton in both world wars. See Lawrence Bergreen, *As Thousands Cheer: The Life of Irving Berlin* (New York: Viking, 1990), chap. 8.

2. General J. Franklin Bell (1856–1919) joined the 7th Cavalry in 1878 after Custer's Last Stand and enjoyed a distinguished military career that included winning the Congressional Medal of Honor during the Philippine insurrection, service as army chief of staff in 1906–10, and training the 77th Division at Camp Upton.

3. The Selective Service Act of 1917 provided for exemption of conscientious objectors who were members of "any well recognized religious sect . . . whose existing creed or principles forbid its members to participate in war in any form." Altogether 3,989 draftees persisted in their claims for objections, of whom 2,599 accepted the alternative of noncombatant service.

4. Father Dunne was subsequently awarded the Distinguished Service Cross during the Argonne offensive for "constantly expos[ing] himself to the heaviest fire in order to assist the wounded men of his regiment, at all times displaying heroic conduct and superb devotion to his duty. His splendid and consistent bravery and contempt for his own safety was a continuing inspiration to every man of his regiment." Quoted in Adler, *History of the 306th*.

5. "Keep your health and your sense of humor," Vidmer advised, "and the rest will take care of itself." Quoted in Adler, *History of the 306th*.

6. "Their heads covered by the winter caps were held high and their fixed bayonets glistened in a never-to-be-forgotten sight. The band played 'Stars and Stripes Forever,' 'The National Emblem March,' and other stirring tunes. Snow began to fall in great fleecy flakes as the squads formed, and the men marched for miles under a canopy of white, while a white blanket muffled their tread and white flakes touched their shoulder lightly as though in benediction." Quoted in Adler, *History of the 306th*. Another officer recalled: "Camp Upton was proud of what it had produced, only regretting that it had to court-martial so many of its members immediately thereafter for lack of a proper sense of when the festivities were over." W. Kerr Rainsford, *From Upton to the Meuse with the Three Hundred and Seventh Infantry* (New York: D. Appleton, 1920), 15.

7. For the problems created by soldiers going AWOL just before embarkation, see Keene, *Doughboys,* 70–72.

The Ocean and England

1. British Prime Minister David Lloyd George had prophesied that America's contribution to victory would be "found in one word, ships, in a second word, ships, and a third

word, ships." Quoted in Frederick Paxson, *American Democracy and the World War* (Boston: Houghton Mifflin, 1936-48), 2:66.

2. Another soldier assigned to the lower quarters recalled: "I'm sure no soldiers ever had as bad accommodations on any other transport. . . . Hammocks were provided for sleeping, but even with two layers there was not enough room and some of the men had to sleep on the wooden tables used for eating. . . . Backless wooden benches were attached to the tables. The food for the men was pretty terrible, and the process of serving it even worse. . . . The whole ship reeked of curry." *World War I Experiences of Talbot M. Brewer,* http://www.longwood.k12.ny.us/history/upton/brewer.htm.

3. "Steering zigzag courses in formation under these conditions with the great unwieldy vessels one thousand yards apart," wrote Captain William D. Leahy, "left very few dull moments for the [escorting] skipper." Altogether, 2,060,000 American troops arrived in France prior to the armistice, of whom 952,000 were transported on American ships. Quoted in Robert H. Ferrell, *Woodrow Wilson and World War I, 1917–1921* (New York: Harper & Row, 1985), 38–39.

4. Fast destroyers based in Queenstown, Ireland, generally joined convoys for the last three hundred to four hundred miles and protected transports from lurking German U-boats.

5. One of the *Karoa*'s passengers recalled: "All [of us] were feeling quite heroic until some wounded Tommies shouted at us: 'Where have you blokes been for the last three years.'" *Experiences of Talbot M. Brewer.*

With the British in Flanders

1. For an excellent discussion of the two AEF divisions that eventually fought under British command in 1918, see Mitchell A. Yorkelson, *Borrowed Soldiers: Americans under British Command, 1918* (Norman: University of Oklahoma Press, 2008).

2. By May 1918 there were 650,000 American soldiers in France, but "to some Frenchmen, it appeared that they had arrived just in time to witness the collapse of a nation." Edward M. Coffman, *The War to End All Wars* (New York: Oxford University Press, 1968), 213.

3. The Germans still held air superiority in May 1918, but the intermittent bombing and strafing tactics of the Great War were far less bothersome to the foot soldiers below than they would be in World War II. See Coffman, *War to End All Wars,* chap. 7.

4. "Blighty" was slang for England.

5. The British Tommies reportedly gave the doughboys sensible advice: "Don't stir up Jerry, Yank; you shoot at im, he'll shoot back." Quoted in Yorkelson, *Borrowed Soldiers,* 87.

6. "Our visiting officers found that the Englishman would not give up his tea habit and at four o'clock he stopped fighting. He must have his tea! The *Boche* was a most discourteous fellow for interrupting this national custom." Adler, *History of the 306th.*

7. For a discussion on how American doughboys and British Tommies "only thought they spoke the same language," see Laurence Stallings, *The Doughboys* (New York: Harper & Row, 1965), 259–60.

8. Robert Graves told a similar story, probably apocryphal, about using heated machine-gun water for tea in *Goodbye to All That* (1929). See Bond, *Survivors of a Kind,* 3.

9. Doughboys also called "Minnie Werfer" the "Iron Mermaid" because of a fishlike tail that kept its trajectory straight. See Slofkin, *Lost Battalions,* 198.

10. "It all began at once," another captain in the 77th Division wrote of his first artillery barrage, "as if at one moment an organist had pulled out all the stops, pressed down all the keys, and stepped hard on all the pedals." Quoted in Sterba, *Good Americans,* 182–83.

11. See "Rare Edition of English Poets Given Library in Memory of Lionel Harvard," *Harvard Crimson*, March 3, 1926.

12. Another veteran of the 306th Infantry wrote that the Watten march "couldn't have been a worse mess for the Division and the [Machine Gun] Company.... Little or no food was supplied, long march, very hot weather, men dropping out.... [We] started our hike back to camp at 1 a.m., and arrived at dawn with men's morale at zero." *Experiences of Talbot M. Brewer*.

13. These were the notorious "40-and-8's"—tiny "French railway freight cars supposedly able to carry 40 men or 8 horses." Doughboys despised them. David M. Kennedy, *Over Here: The First World War and American Society*, 25th anniversary ed. (New York: Oxford University Press, 2004), 189.

The Baccarat Sector

1. The day after the 306th Regiment arrived, a German plane flew over and dropped leaflets that read: "Good-by 42nd Division. Hello 77th." Quoted in Adler, *History of the 306th*.

2. Adler, who became vice president of the *New York Times* between the wars, served as the commanding general of the 77th Division in World War II.

The Vesle Sector

1. A recent historian of the AEF notes that the 77th Division suffered fourteen hundred casualties in its first week on the Vesle: "The incessant artillery fire, frequent gas attacks, occasional enemy raids, lack of adequate trenches and dugouts, exposed infantry detachments, and a policy of aggressive patrolling all contributed to the high casualty figure. Soon, the men of the 77th Division were calling the sector 'the Hell-hole Valley of the Vesle.'" Mark E. Grotelueschen, *The AEF Way of War* (New York: Cambridge University Press, 2006), 290.

2. Talbot Brewer noticed the wrecks of two American planes near Fère-en-Tardenois, "one of which belonged to Quentin Roosevelt," Theodore Roosevelt's son. *Experiences of Talbot M. Brewer*.

3. Doughboys would soon call the Vesle sector "Death Valley." Quoted in Allen R. Millett, *The General: Robert L. Bullard and Officership in the United States Army, 1881–1925* (Westport, Conn.: Greenwood Press, 1975), 386.

4. Patterson and his doughboys were experiencing what historian Peter Kindsvatter calls "green-unit eagerness to come to grips with the Hun," an overconfidence that was quickly dispelled by the exigencies of combat. Peter E. Kindsvatter, *American Soldiers: Ground Combat in the World Wars, Korea, & Vietnam* (Lawrence: University Press of Kansas, 2003), 69–70.

5. "Showing an utter disregard for their own safety," Thacher, Patterson, and the other officers "calmly walked among the men indicating to each soldier the best method for seeking shelter." Adler, *History of the 306th*.

6. Intelligence reported at least thirty-seven German machine gun nests operating inside Bazoches.

7. Patterson later reported that Private Charles W. Wogatzke was "buried August 14th 1918 in a small clump of trees beside a lagoon called 'La Graviere' about 300 yards north of the Vesle and ½ mile west of Bazoches. The grave was marked." Patterson affidavit for American Grave Registration Service, March 13, 1926, Robert P. Patterson MSS, Library of Congress, Washington, D.C.

8. According to journalist Forrest Davis, "Every insect known to the French countryside advanced to the attack, reminding their victim of Gulliver's treatment at the hands of the Lilliputians. Unwilling to move a muscle, Patterson thought longingly of the filled water canteen by his side. A man of weaker nervous organization would have risen, screaming, and dashed to his death. Not Patterson. He remained prone and motionless until ten p.m., when darkness justified a sprint through the murk. He . . . reckoned that his luck would hold. It did." Davis, "Toughest Man," 60.

9. Patterson subsequently recommended "Dick" Foy for a job with the *New York Times* and later helped him become a deputy clerk at the U.S. District Court, Southern District of New York, in the 1930s. Finucane became a bakery executive after the war, John Duffy a bank guard, and Samuel Silverstein a tailor. Finucane called Patterson "the most modest and bravest of men I have ever met." See *New York Times*, July 10, 1952, clipping in possession of Virginia Montgomery. Patterson to Julius Adler, April 20, 1936, and Adler to Patterson, April 21, 1936, Patterson MSS. Communication from Robert P. Patterson Jr., November 7, 2010.

10. After the war Patterson also praised Sergeant Michael Connolly as "one of the best soldiers who ever wore a uniform. He went up from private to corporal, and from corporal to sergeant, all in the month we spent on the Vesle. He proved himself fearless in action and a hard worker in every way." Patterson to Julius Adler, January 22, 1923, Patterson MSS.

11. Patterson left modest bequests to his rescuers in his will. Eiler, *Mobilizing America*, 22–23. In later recommending his men for the Distinguished Service Cross, Patterson described their rescue efforts as "the most daring piece of work that I witnessed in the whole war. The circumstances are particularly striking when it is remembered that these men were raw soldiers, this being only their second day in an active sector, and that all of them voluntarily undertook those hazards." Patterson to Colonel George Vidmer, March 31, 1923, Patterson MSS. See also *New York Times*, July 10, 1952.

12. General Pershing would later write laconically: "The 77th Division took over the front of the 4th Division in the I Corps near Bazoches on August 12th. Elements . . . succeeded in crossing the Vesle River, encountering tenacious defense." John J. Pershing, *My Experiences in the World War* (New York: Frederick A. Stokes, 1931), vol. 2:210–11.

13. Patterson was lucky to have survived with only minor effects. A British nurse described the victims of mustard gas: "the poor things burnt and blistered all over with great mustard-coloured suppurating blisters, with blind eyes . . . all sticky and stuck together, and always fighting for breath, with voices a mere whisper, saying that their throats were closing and they know they will choke. The only good thing one can say is that such severe cases don't last long." Vera Brittain, *Testament of Youth* (New York: Macmillan, 1933), 395.

14. Several years later Patterson reported to the quartermaster general's office the approximate location of Byrne's grave along the railroad tracks, "about a half mile west of the railroad station at Bazoches." Patterson to War Department, March 12, 1926, Patterson MSS.

15. After the war Patterson interceded with the Veterans Bureau and Red Cross to seek medical insurance and treatment for Private Henry Mooso, also severely gassed near Bazoches at this time. Patterson to Margaret Dyer, March 2, 1922, Patterson MSS.

16. Roger Lapham was a Harvard graduate and later mayor of San Francisco, 1944–48.

17. The official history of the 77th Division describes the assault on Bazoches: "The attack started at 4:15 a.m. supported by artillery and machine-gun barrages. The town was entered but after heavy losses the troops were forced to return to their original positions." American Battle Monuments Commission, *77th Division: Summary of Operations in the World War* (Washington, D.C.: Government Printing Office, 1944), 10.

18. Colonel Adler would also write: "After mature reflection, one is led to believe, knowing the almost impregnable positions of the many machine-gun nests in the town, that no less than a regiment could have taken it and held it against the hostile counter-attacks." Adler, *History of the 306th*.

19. Beginning on October 2, 1917, units of the 307th and 308th Infantry Regiments, plus two companies of the 306th Machine Gun Battalion, advanced into the Argonne Forest much more quickly than American forces on their right flank and French units on their left. Cut off, surrounded, and outnumbered by counterattacking German forces, the so-called "Lost Battalion" suffered heavy losses and many hardships, including dwindling supplies, scarce food and water, and "friendly" American artillery bombardment aimed at the wrong targets. Carrier pigeons became the only means of outside communication. One of these pigeons, appropriately named Cher Ami, finally summoned relief from Allied units after five harrowing days. Only 194 out of more than five hundred doughboys walked out of "the pocket" unscathed. Major Charles W. Whittlesey and six others would receive the Congressional Medal of Honor for their heroism. Nonetheless, burdened by the loss of so many of his men, Whittlesey committed suicide in 1921. See Robert H. Ferrell, *Five Days in October: The Lost Battalion of World War I* (Columbia: University of Missouri Press, 2005).

The Aisne

1. The official summary states: "On September 5 possession of the plateau between the Vesle and Aisne rivers was secured. The following week was marked by frequent local actions which resulted in minor changes in the front." *77th Division*, 7.

2. General Alexander had ordered that patrols "be pushed aggressively across the Aisne and establish themselves on the heights" above the river. He even urged infantry to "swim across if necessary." According to Mark Grotelueschen, "this was all completely unrealistic . . . without prearranged artillery fire." Quoted in *AEF Way of War*, 303.

3. U.S. artillery had battered Bazoches from August 30 until September 4. "The town was hammered, stone from stone, until . . . no buildings, and only part of the church, were at all intact." Adler, *History of the Seventy-seventh*, 45.

4. Patterson may also have picked up a German helmet here that he later brought home to his family. Indeed, doughboys earned a reputation for being inveterate souvenir hunters: As one jokester put it, England fought for "freedom of the seas; France for La Patrie; U.S. for souvenirs." Quoted in Kindsvatter, *American Soldiers*, 266.

5. "We were relieved that night by an Italian Division who came through Fisme and across the Vesle with an incredible amount of noise—lanterns, cigarettes, matches, everything but a brass band. For the first time in two weeks there was no shelling. On any previous night they would have been cut to pieces." *Experiences of Talbot M. Brewer*. "General Garibaldi, a grandson of the Italian liberator, was in command of the relieving division, every member of which wore a red silk handkerchief in the upper right-hand pocket of his uniform, a gift of an American woman." Adler, *History of the Seventy-seventh*, 58.

The Argonne

1. General Hunter Liggett famously described the Argonne Forest as a "long and narrow wood running roughly north and south and not unlike, in shape and position, Manhattan Island." Hunter S. Liggett, *AEF: Ten Years Ago in France* (New York: Dodd, Mead, 1928), 167.

2. One scholar writes: "The poor road network that ran along the west bank of the Meuse, the broken nature of the terrain, the maze of German entrenchments, and the cratered landscape . . . combined to make even the simplest movements difficult. To compound these problems, the weather turned bad. Heavy rains began to fall on the first day of the battle and swiftly turned the three narrow roads, the only routes of communication into this sector, into quagmires." Robert B. Bruce, *A Fraternity of Arms: America & France in the Great War* (Lawrence: University Press of Kansas, 2003), 270.

3. A surgeon in the AEF medical corps described the movements of troops on the night before the Argonne attack: "Prowling, skulking, preparing, stalking, 500,000 armed human beings accompanied by acres of guns—paraphernalia covering the earth—a blanket of destruction ten miles deep, thirty miles long, gliding by inches, skulking by inches—hundreds of thousands of my fellow beings are dragging and lugging this vast carpet of destruction toward the enemy." George Crile quoted in Robert H. Ferrell, *America's Deadliest Battle: Meuse-Argonne, 1918* (Columbia: University of Missouri Press, 2007), 39.

4. "The average doughboy at the Meuse-Argonne had seen perhaps four months of training in camp. Many had seen but a few weeks. Some had been cycled so swiftly from induction center to war zone that they had never handled a rifle, and had to be given a quick ten-day course of instruction upon arrival in France." Kennedy, *Over Here*, 199.

5. Robert Alexander, 1863–1941. Born in Maryland, Alexander enlisted in the army as a private in 1886 and rose through the ranks with service in the Indian campaign of 1890–91, the Spanish-American War, the Philippine insurrection, and the Mexican campaign of 1916. In France he commanded the 41st Division before taking over the 77th. Alexander retired a major general in 1927 and his *Memories of the World War, 1917–1918* (New York: Macmillan, 1931) ranks among the best first-hand accounts.

6. "3,800 guns ranging from 75 mm. to enormous American-made 14-inch railroad guns opened fire with a crash. More ammunition was expended during this preparation fire than was used by both sides during the entire Civil War—and at a cost estimated at a million dollars a minute." John Toland, *No Man's Land: 1918, the Last Year of the Great War* (Garden City, N.Y.: Doubleday, 1980), 431.

7. Another veteran of the 77th division described the terrain that lay ahead: "a bleak, cruel country of white clay and rock and blasted skeletons of trees, gashed into innumerable trenches, and seared with rusted acres of wires, rising steeply into claw-like ridges and descending into haunted ravines, white as leprosy in the midst of that green forest, a country that had died long ago, and in pain." W. Kerr Rainsford, *From Upton to the Meuse with the Three Hundred and Seventh Infantry* (New York: Appleton, 1920), 158–59.

8. General Liggett recalled: "The miserable roads began to have their effect on the second day. As the infantry advanced it lost the proper support of the artillery, which was unable to follow. The engineers and pioneers toiled furiously, but their task was an appalling one. Four years of shell fire had left the spongy soil of No Man's Land a troubled sea. . . . [A] succession of half-obliterated trenches, water-filled shell holes and tangles of wire defied transport; and when the artillery did slug its way through, it found itself at a disadvantage, at first, in the blind country." Liggett, *AEF,* 178–79.

9. General Alexander of the 77th Division considered "old Wit" his most effective commander. Quoted in Robert H. Ferrell, ed., *In the Company of Generals: The World War I Diary of Pierrepont L. Stackpole* (Columbia: University of Missouri Press, 2009), 158.

10. Another doughboy of the 77th Division commented: "Even more depressing than the lack of vision . . . was the dank breath of the Argonne, saturated, until by dawn the atmosphere had passed mellowness, with the odor of stagnant, muddy pools, hiding beneath treacherous carpets of tangled wire grass and bringing to the nostrils . . . a reminder of the

awful slaughter which had left another carpet on this mutilated soil [two years earlier] when a barrier of horizon-blue *poilus* had hurled back the Crown Prince's army." L. Wardlaw Miles, *History of the 308th Infantry* (New York: G. P. Putnam's Sons, 1927), 123.

11. Patterson's hot meal in the midst of battle may have been an exception. British Field Marshal Sir Douglas Haig's diary for October 4, 1918, reads: "He [Marshal Foch] was very disappointed with the American attack west of the Meuse. Many of their divisions had been several days without food. Some had run off to get something to eat." Quoted in Harvey A. DeWeerd, *President Wilson Fights His War* (New York: Macmillan, 1968), 347.

12. General Alexander estimated that ten Americans were lost for every German killed in the first days of the Meuse-Argonne offensive. Alexander, *Memories,* 190.

13. General Pershing's biographer notes: "The transportation problem was such that, quite literally, the AEF threatened to become immobile. A huge mass of men and matériel, it would soon be like a giant turtle tipped over on its back, floundering helplessly, unable to move." Donald M. Smythe, *Pershing: General of the Armies* (Bloomington: Indiana University Press, 1986), 207.

14. General Pershing visited the front on September 28 and learned in detail about the harsh "terrain, the insidious nature of the opposition, and the handicap all divisions suffered by reason of inexperience, lack of training, new officers, losses of officers, and poor ones. Pershing said he appreciated this . . . and seemed to be in good enough humor." Quoted in Ferrell, *Company of Generals,* 146.

15. Patterson may have mistaken the date. According to the official summary, "at 1:15 a.m. the 153d Infantry Brigade issued orders for the 306th Infantry to relieve the 305th Infantry during the night of October 5-6. At about 6 p.m. the 306th Infantry commenced taking over the front line, completing the relief about 9 p.m." *77th Division,* 54.

16. Patterson described the ensuing action for the Battle Monuments Commission: "In the morning of October 7th an attack was made by the entire Battalion. . . . Except for the first hundred yards or so there was no fighting, and at dark on October 7th this Company was dug in along the road from Binarville to la Viergette and the narrow gauge railway along the road. . . . On October 8th we advanced about a kilometer, without resistance On October 9th this Battalion advanced about four kilometers . . . without serious resistance. On October 10th the advance was resumed with this Battalion on the front line of the Regiment. . . . Company F was on the right of the Battalion Center, and one platoon occupied Chevieres, which was then burning. This was a permanent occupation, and a platoon of the 307th Infantry relieved us there on the morning of October 11th." Patterson report to Battle Monuments Commission, March 12, 1926, Patterson MSS.

17. Patterson is referring here to "stragglers," a euphemism for deserters. General Hunter Liggett estimated nearly 100,000 such laggards during the Meuse-Argonne battle and therefore ordered "straggler's posts on all the roads, tightened the military policing of back areas and sent out officers with patrols to search the woods and dugouts, and thousands of strays and hideaways poured in." Quoted in David F. Trask, *The AEF and Coalition Warmaking, 1917–1918* (Lawrence: University Press of Kansas, 1993), 146.

18. Future Congressman Maury Maverick of Texas also endured artillery bombardment at this time: "There is a great swishing scream, a smash-bang, and it seems to tear everything loose from you. The intensity of it simply enters your heart and brain, and tears every nerve to pieces." Quoted in Coffman, *War to End All Wars,* 322.

19. Historian Edward Lengel writes that the 306th Infantry had misconstrued orders by marching toward the riverbank too close to St. Juvin. "The mistake had terrible consequences. There was no cover at that point on the riverbank. Worse, there was no way to cross. Instead of withdrawing, the battalion commander held his men in full view of the

enemy while the scouts ran back and forth, desperately trying find a place to bridge or ford. German artillery and machine guns on the high ground north of the river methodically ravaged the battalion until it practically disintegrated, at which time its commander pulled it back to a more sheltered position and dug in." Lengel, *To Conquer Hell*, 343.

20. Patterson took a personal interest after the war in getting medical treatment from the Veterans Bureau for Jacob Drabkin, who "was severely wounded in the right thigh. The wound occurred in my presence and I personally bandaged his leg, so I am personally familiar with all the circumstances. The fact that he received this wound was duly noted on his discharge papers. The wound is plainly visible on his right thigh, the scar being about five inches by two inches. It is a plain case of a wound received in action, and I cannot understand the total failure of the Bureau to take any action on the matter." Patterson to Veterans Bureau, May 3, 1922, Patterson MSS.

21. Private Arthur T. Ulness witnessed the death of his brother, Private Oscar E. Ulness.

22. In an account of his friend's death written in 1931, Patterson noted that "I had just run down the hill myself, having arranged with Hayes to send the men forward upon signal from myself. He came down the hill himself, either to tell me something or because of his impatience not to be well in front." Patterson to Julius Adler, May 27, 1931, Patterson MSS.

23. Captain Julius O. Adler and two soldiers from Company H proceeded to "shoot up the town like a bunch of cowboys at the end of a cattle drive, giving the impression that a larger force than three isolated Doughboys was advancing." Eventually fifty Germans surrendered, and another one hundred fled. Stallings, *The Doughboys*, 330.

24. After capturing St. Juvin, Adler and two of his men chased retreating Germans toward the nearby Hill 182, where "another 150 or so enemy soldiers stood bewildered on the crest. Audaciously, Adler and the two other Americans climbed the hill, firing at the Germans above them. Joined by a Chauchat team and another group of ten soldiers, they closed within point-blank range. Incredibly, the enemy soldiers—who outnumbered the attackers by about ten to one—waved white flags or fled." Lengel, *To Conquer Hell*, 344–45.

25. Such a graphic description would never have passed the wartime censors. According to the War Department, photographs of dead or wounded Americans "caused needless anxiety to those whose friends or relatives were at the front." Quoted in Susan A. Brewer, *Why America Fights* (New York: Oxford University Press, 2009), 73.

26. One AEF chaplain tried to comfort a wounded doughboy who had lost an eye, by saying: "Uncle Sam will look after you." The soldier replied: "I'm not thinking about Uncle Sam at all. There's a girl back in New York who doesn't care whether I have one eye or two." Quoted in Kindsvatter, *American Soldiers*, 122.

27. AEF veteran and future historian William L. Langer later wrote that artillery shell fire "always seemed a bit unfair to me. Somehow it makes one feel so helpless, there is no chance of reprisal for the individual man. The advantage is all with the shell, and you have no comeback." Langer, *Gas and Flame in World War I* (New York: A. P. Knopf, 1965), 24.

28. In an account written for the Battle Monuments Commission in 1930, Patterson described the fighting on October 15: "Before dawn my company crossed the Aire River southeast of St. Juvin, the bulk of our regiment having already crossed. About dawn I found the battalion commander (Major A. G. Thacher) with E Company and G Company on the reverse slope about half a kilometer east of St. Juvin, just north of the St. Juvin–Fleville road. Several companies of the first battalion of our regiment were also on this reverse slope (I remember seeing men of A Company and B Company there), and there were also some companies of the 305th Infantry a short distance to the east on the same reverse slope. At this place I saw Captain Prentice of the 308th Infantry, with a small patrol. He told us that

our left flank was left entirely unprotected and that there were no Americans to the west of the town. Very severe shelling took place just after dawn, which caused considerable confusion among the companies upon the reverse slope, most of the men trying to get to the steepest places. When the shelling stopped, I and several others saw a party of Germans, probably 20 or 30 men at our left rear, moving about on a small hill or ridge just south of St. Juvin. Major Thacher ordered me to drive this party off at once. I collected one platoon of my company and advanced on the hill at double time, keeping up a steady fire with rifles and Chauchat rifles, and receiving machine gun fire from the hill and also from the houses at the south end of the town. The German fire was not heavy. I was supported on the left by a platoon of G Company under Lieutenant Henry, these troops crossing the low valley nearer the ridge. Before we reached the hill, the Germans ran away to the southeast. We found two dead in a machine gun pit on the hill; the houses were found to be empty. We were then joined by the other three platoons and spent some time roaming around the town and the country just to the west of it without results. There were no Americans to the west of the town. I then received orders to return to the reverse slope east of St. Juvin." Patterson report to Battle Monuments Commission, March 17, 1930, Patterson MSS.

29. When Thacher was awarded the Distinguished Service Cross in 1922, Patterson wrote to him: "There were so many occasions during August, September, and October of 1918, on which your conduct had won the admiration of everyone near you, that it would be hard to say which one had been singled out. I particularly had in mind the fracas on the Vesle, the reconnaissance you made on the Aisne, the patrol which you had opposite Grandpre, and the attack on St. Juvin. This really gives me more satisfaction than anything that has happened since the war." Patterson to Archibald Thacher, October 21, 1922, Patterson MSS.

30. U.S. soldiers sang a variation of the 1918 popular song "K-K-K-Katy, Beautiful Katy"—"C-C-C-Cootie, / Horrible cootie, / You're the only b-b-b-bug that I abhor; / When the m-m-moon shines over the bunkhouse, / I will scratch my b-b-b-back until it's sore." Quoted in Mark Sullivan, *Our Times: The United States, 1900-1925* (New York: Charles Scribner's Sons, 1933), 5:338. Another doughboy used the "kerosene cure." "By the time I had my clothes on again I was in agony. The stuff burned like fire, and for the rest of the day I roamed around like a dog with a can tied to its tail. It didn't kill the cooties either." Horatio Rogers quoted in Kindsvatter, *American Soldiers,* 43.

31. Because the YMCA operated all the post exchanges for the AEF and profited from selling cigarettes that were supposed to be gifts, the doughboys often used profanity when referring to "that damn Y." Katherine Mayo, *"That Damn Y": A Record of Overseas Service* (Boston: Houghton Mifflin, 1920).

32. Patterson does not mention the favorite song of doughboys in France, one of the milder versions of which goes: "Oh, Mademoiselle from Armentieres, / Parlez-vous? / Oh, Mademoiselle from Armentieres, / Parlez-vous? / You didn't have to know her long, / To know the reason men go wrong! / Hinky-dinky, parlez-vous?" Quoted in Lengel, *To Conquer Hell,* 67. Virginia Montgomery recalls that her father did teach her the chorus.

33. Despite Patterson's positive view of General Alexander, the most recent historian of the Meuse-Argonne battle concludes that Alexander "was no leader. Brash and sarcastic, Alexander heaped responsibilities on subordinates and infuriated them with constant prodding. As an administrator and strategist he was mediocre. A firm believer in Pershing's doctrine of rifle and bayonet over massed firepower, he regularly disregarded the importance of artillery." Lengel, *To Conquer Hell,* 118.

34. The German retreat in the last days before the armistice still took its toll on advancing doughboys. The novelist F. Scott Fitzgerald would write that the enemy "walked very

slowly backward, a few inches a day, leaving the dead like a million bloody rags." Quoted in Byron Farwell, *Over There: The United States in the Great War, 1917–1918* (New York: W. W. Norton, 1999), 241.

35. A doughboy entering one abandoned house found a sign in English, "For Officers Only," along with two pistols and several German helmets. A second sign read: "Souvenirs for you Americans. We'll be home for Christmas and you won't." Adler, *History of the Seventy-seventh,* 91.

36. Another U.S. soldier described the "steady knife-edge wind of November" as "pure agony. It drives inside to meet the chills deep in your bone and makes you shake. Your lower jaw trembles like a loose-hinged gate until you can lash it fast with your helmet strap, pulling your face together to stop the chattering of your teeth." Quoted in Kindsvatter, *American Soldiers,* 43.

37. The official history of the 77th Division notes that on November 5, the "1st Battalion, 306th Infantry, was held up in Bois de Franclieu by artillery fire and reached the vicinity of Le Franc Lieu Ferme shortly before 4 p.m." *77th Division,* 92.

38. An engineer in the 77th Division later wrote: "The advance of the Division from the early morning of the 2nd of November to the evening of the 6th was the most rapid in its history." Quoted in Ferrell, *America's Deadliest Battle,* 138.

39. Another doughboy in the 77th Division recalled that the people in Le Besace "consisted of women, old men and very small children and it is quite possible that some of those children may have been German. . . . Those poor French people were uncertain whether or not to be afraid of us." Henry W. Smith, *A Story of the 305th Machine Gun Battalion, 77th Division A.E.F.* (New York: Modern Composing Room, 1941), 76–77.

40. As one general put it, the armistice would prevent American soldiers from "planting my hob-nailed boots on German soil." Quoted in Heath Twichell Jr., *Allen: The Biography of an Army Officer, 1859–1930* (New Brunswick, N.J.: Rutgers University Press, 1974), 211.

41. The German General Erich von Ludendorff would later write: "It was most assuredly the Americans who bore the heaviest brunt of the fighting on the whole battle front during the last few months of the war," and German forces were unable to "withstand the incessant force of intrepidity of the American attack." Erich Ludendorff and others, *The Two Battles of the Marne* (New York: Cosmopolitan, 1927), 228. Edward Lengel offers a more nuanced judgment: The AEF "had not won the war, but it had appreciably helped to hasten its end, and it had accomplished the limits of which it, or practically any other army, was capable under the circumstances. That was much more than the French could have done in its place, and about equal to what the British could have achieved—albeit with a smaller casualty list." Lengel, *To Conquer Hell,* 420.

After the Armistice

1. "Over on the German side of the Meuse, some Very pistol man continued to send up rockets in groups of three—a red, a white, and a blue. This was taken by the Americans as an effort on the part of the Germans, who now saw that their fate was sealed, to fraternize with the Yankee soldier—and the incident was ignored. The absence of planes, the big guns not roaring, and the rifles not cracking, put a mysterious touch into life at the front that night. The whole battlefield seemed deserted." Adler, *History of the Seventy-seventh,* 100.

2. General Pershing was disappointed that the armistice had come before the AEF had invaded Germany. "I suppose our campaigns have ended," he said, "but what an enormous difference a few days more would have made." Quoted in John S. D. Eisenhower, *Yanks: The Epic Story of the American Army in World War I* (New York: Free Press, 2001), 283.

3. Middleton was a close friend and fellow editor with Patterson of the *Harvard Law Review* in 1914–15.

4. Jennifer Keene notes that "until a peace treaty was signed, the army wanted to maintain an obedient, combat-ready force." Keene, *Doughboys*, 134.

5. After the war, when Carroll earned a citation for heroism as a New York City firefighter, Patterson wrote to the fire chief that Carroll "was without question the bravest soldier I have ever known. . . . Nothing in my life has given me greater pleasure than to see Carroll come back from the hospital six months later, in as good a shape as if he had not been hit." Patterson to John Kenlon, February 19, 1926, Patterson MSS.

6. Patterson later pressed the Veterans Bureau for disability payments to Corporal Lewis for wounds to his "buttocks, thigh, and ankle, and the three machine-gun bullets [that] are still in his body." Patterson to Veterans Bureau, June 20, 1927, Patterson MSS.

7. Patterson's regiment seems to have escaped the ravages of the Spanish influenza pandemic that killed more than 57,000 American soldiers in 1918–19. See Carol R. Byerly, *Fever of War: The Influenza Epidemic in the U.S. Army in World War I* (New York: New York University Press, 2005).

8. During the 1920s and 1930s Patterson performed numerous legal services for "Sammy" Silverstein, for whom he had the "highest regard." Among other favors he helped Silverstein obtain a license to sell poultry. When Silverstein's business went bankrupt, Patterson fashioned an arrangement whereby he would pay off his creditors gradually but at "100 cents to the dollar." See Silverstein to Patterson, June 22, 1922, and Patterson to Silverstein, March 29, 1924, Patterson MSS. Also Robert P. Patterson Jr. e-mail to J. G. Clifford, June 27, 2010. Patterson's enduring friendships with Silverstein, Jacob Drabkin, and other Jewish doughboys partly mitigate Richard Slotkin's judgment that the Lower East Side immigrants of the "Lost Battalion" endured anti-Semitic WASP disapproval after the World War I. See Slotkin, *Lost Battalions*, 453–61.

9. In recommending Ruppertsburg for a job after the war, Patterson would write: "In addition to possessing all the usual qualities that make an excellent soldier, Ruppertsburg had an unfailing sense of humor that made him, in my opinion, the most valuable man in the Company in keeping up a high morale." Patterson to H. T. Partridge, June 21, 1924, Patterson MSS.

10. Patterson and his wife Margaret visited France again in the summer of 1924. "We bought bicycles and rode about quite a bit. The trips to the old sectors where I had been in the war were quite interesting, but the best features proved to be our visits to the villages behind the lines where I had stayed after the armistice and where I knew all the people." Patterson to L. F. Hyde, October 14, 1924, Patterson MSS.

Infantry Equipment and Tactics

1. Patterson's determination that American soldiers should have the best combat weapons later embroiled him in controversy as assistant secretary of war in favoring adoption of the Garand semiautomatic rifle in 1940–41. Eiler, *Mobilizing America*, 115–20.

2. One historian notes: "Bayonets were the most overrated weapon of the war, and AEF surgeons saw almost no bayonet wounds because attacking troops could not get close enough to the enemy to use them, especially if the defenders possessed machine guns. Bayonets had only two uses: to hang gear on and to dig foxholes when shovels were not available." Ferrell, *America's Deadliest Battle*, 15.

3. With respect to the fighting in Vesle and Aisne sectors, a lieutenant in the 306th Machine Gun Battalion later observed: "The liaison between Corps, Division H.Q., Brigade

H.Q., Regimental H.Q., and down to the poor Infantry Battalions and Companies who had to do the actual attacking was incredibly bad. Orders reached the Battalions and Companies far too late, if at all, to stage the coordinated attacks contemplated by the higher echelons. Consequently, the attacks were made in driblets, one or two Companies at a time, with little, if any, artillery preparation and were completely futile." *Experiences of Talbot M. Brewer.*

4. In the Meuse-Argonne offensive of September–November 1918, the 306th Infantry suffered 186 deaths. See *77th Division,* 104.

Bibliography

Adler, Julius O. *History of the Seventy-seventh Division: August 25th, 1917, November 11th, 1918*. New York: 77th Infantry Association, 1919.

Adler, Julius O. *History of the 305th Infantry*. New York, 1935. http://www.longwood.k12.ny.us/history/upton/adler/adler.htm.

Alexander, Robert. *Memories of the World War, 1917–1918*. New York: Macmillan, 1931.

American Battle Monuments Commission. *77th Division: Summary of Operations in the World War*. Washington, D.C.: Government Printing Office, 1944.

Bergreen, Lawrence. *As Thousands Cheer: The Life of Irving Berlin*. New York: Viking, 1990.

Bond, Brian. *Survivors of a Kind: Memoirs of the Western Front*. New York & London: Continuum, 2008.

Brewer, Susan A. *Why America Fights*. New York: Oxford University Press, 2009.

Brewer, Talbot. *World War I Experiences of Talbot M. Brewer*. http://www.longwood.k12.ny.us/history/upton/brewer.htm.

Brittain, Vera. *Testament of Youth*. New York: Macmillan, 1933.

Bruce, Robert B. *A Fraternity of Arms: America & France in the Great War*. Lawrence: University Press of Kansas, 2003.

Bundy, McGeorge, and Henry L. Stimson. *On Active Service in Peace and War*. New York: Harper & Brothers, 1947.

Byerly, Carol R. *Fever of War: The Influenza Epidemic in the U.S. Army in World War I*. New York: New York University Press, 2005.

Clifford, J. Garry, and Samuel R. Spencer Jr. *The First Peacetime Draft*. Lawrence: University Press of Kansas, 1986.

Clifford, John Garry. *The Citizen Soldiers: The Plattsburg Training Camp Movement, 1913–1920*. Lexington: University Press of Kentucky, 1972.

Coffman, Edward M. *The Regulars: The American Army, 1898–1941*. Cambridge, Mass.: Harvard University Press, 2004.

———. *The War to End All Wars*. New York: Oxford University Press, 1968.

Dalfiume, Richard M. *Desegregation of the Armed Forces*. Columbia: University of Missouri Press, 1969.

Davis, Forrest. "The Toughest Man in Washington." *Saturday Evening Post*, September 5, 1942.

DeWeerd, Harvey A. *President Wilson Fights His War*. New York: Macmillan, 1968.

Eiler, Keith E. *Mobilizing America: Robert P. Patterson and the War Effort 1940–1945*. Ithaca, N.Y.: Cornell University Press, 1997.

Eisenhower, John S. D. *Yanks: The Epic Story of the American Army in World War I*. New York: The Free Press, 2001.

Farwell, Byron. *Over There: The United States in the Great War, 1917–1918.* New York: W. W. Norton, 1999.

Ferrell, Robert H. *America's Deadliest Battle: Meuse-Argonne, 1918.* Columbia: University of Missouri Press, 2007.

———. *Five Days in October: The Lost Battalion of World War I.* Columbia: University of Missouri Press, 2005.

———. *Woodrow Wilson and World War I, 1917–1921.* New York: Harper & Row, 1985.

Ferrell, Robert H., ed. *In the Company of Generals: The World War I Diary of Pierrepont L. Stackpole.* Columbia: University of Missouri Press, 2009.

Finnegan, John P. *Against the Specter of a Dragon: The Campaign for Military Preparedness, 1914–1917.* Westport, Conn.: Greenwood Press, 1974.

Ford, Nancy Gentile. *Americans All: Foreign-Born Soldiers in World War I.* College Station: Texas A&M University Press, 2001.

Fussell, Paul. *The Great War and Modern Memory.* New York: Oxford University Press, 1975.

———. *Wartime.* New York: Oxford University Press, 1989.

Grotelueschen, Mark E. *The AEF Way of War.* New York: Cambridge University Press, 2006.

Karsten, Peter, ed. *The Military in America.* New York: Simon & Schuster, 1980.

Keene, Jennifer D. *Doughboys, the Great War, and the Remaking of America.* Baltimore: Johns Hopkins University Press, 2001.

Kennedy, David M. *Over Here: The First World War and American Society.* 25th anniversary ed. New York: Oxford University Press, 2004.

Kindsvatter, Peter E. *American Soldiers: Ground Combat in the World Wars, Korea & Vietnam.* Lawrence: University Press of Kansas, 2003.

Langer, William L. *Gas and Flame in World War I.* New York: A. P. Knopf, 1965.

Lengel, Edward G. *To Conquer Hell: The Meuse-Argonne, 1918.* New York: Henry Holt, 2008.

———. *World War I Memories.* Lanham, Md..: Scarecrow Press, 2004.

Liggett, Hunter S. *AEF: Ten Years Ago in France.* New York: Dodd, Mead, 1928.

Ludendorff, Erich, and others. *The Two Battles of the Marne.* New York: Cosmopolitan, 1927.

Mayo, Katherine. *"That Damn Y": A Record of Overseas Service.* Boston: Houghton Mifflin, 1920.

Miles, L. Wardlaw. *History of the 308th Infantry.* New York: G. P. Putnam's Sons, 1927.

Millett, Allen R. *The General: Robert L. Bullard and Officership in the United States Army, 1881–1925.* Westport, Conn.: Greenwood Press, 1975.

Paterson, Thomas G., and others. *American Foreign Relations: A History, Volume 2: Since 1895.* 7th ed. Boston: Wadsworth/Cengage, 2010.

Patterson, Robert Porter. Papers in Manuscript Division of the Library of Congress, Washington, D.C.

Paxson, Frederick. *American Democracy and the World War.* 3 vols. Boston: Houghton Mifflin, 1936–48.

Pearlman, Michael. *To Make Democracy Safe for America: Patricians and Preparedness in the Progressive Era.* Urbana: University of Illinois Press, 1984.

Pershing, John J. *My Experiences in the World War.* 2 vols. New York: Frederick A. Stokes, 1931.

Piehler, G. Kurt. *Remembering War the American Way.* Washington, D.C.: Smithsonian Institution Press, 1995.

Rainsford, W. Kerr. *From Upton to the Meuse with the Three Hundred and Seventh Infantry.* New York: D. Appleton, 1920.

Schifferle, Peter J. *America's School for War: Fort Leavenworth, Officer Education, and Victory in World War II.* Lawrence: University Press of Kansas, 2010.

Slotkin, Richard. *Lost Battalions: The Great War and the Crisis of American Nationality.* New York: Henry Holt, 2005.

Smith, Henry W. *A Story of the 305th Machine Gun Battalion, 77th Division A.E.F.* New York: Modern Composing Room, 1941.

Smythe, Donald M. *Pershing: General of the Armies.* Bloomington: Indiana University Press, 1986.

Stallings, Lawrence. *The Doughboys.* New York: Harper & Row, 1965.

Sterba, Christopher M. *Good Americans All: Italian and Jewish Immigrants in the First World War.* New York: Oxford University Press, 2003.

Sullivan, Mark. *Our Times: The United States, 1900–1925.* 6 vols. New York: Charles Scribner's Sons, 1933.

Toland, John. *No Man's Land: 1918, the Last Year of the Great War.* Garden City, N.Y.: Doubleday, 1980.

Trask, David F. *The AEF and Coalition Warmaking, 1917–1918.* Lawrence: University Press of Kansas, 1993.

Trout, Steven. *On the Battlefield of Memory: The First World War and American Remembrance, 1919–1941.* Tuscaloosa: University of Alabama Press, 2010.

Twichell, Heath, Jr. *Allen: The Biography of an Army Officer, 1859–1930.* New Brunswick, N.J.: Rutgers University Press, 1974.

Yorkelson, Mitchell A. *Borrowed Soldiers: Americans under British Command, 1918.* Norman: University of Oklahoma Press, 2008.

Index

Page numbers in **boldface** refer to illustrations.

2nd Division, 71
39th Infantry, 38
42nd (Rainbow) Division, 29
47th Infantry, 38
77-mm Field Gun, **26**
78th Division, 68, 71
155-mm heavy gun, **83**
165th Infantry, 29
305th Infantry, 55, 59, 99n, 100n
306th Infantry, xi–xvi, **xvii**, 12, **46**, 95n, 99n3; casualties in, 103n
306th Machine Gun Battalion, 17, 97n, 103n
307th Infantry, xvi, 85, 99n
308th Infantry, 39, **64**, 97n, 100n

A Company, 51, 56, 100n
Adler, Maj. Julius O., xvi, 36, 69, 9; attack on St. Juvin, 100n; commands 77th Division in World War II, 95n; described by Patterson, 30
Aire River, xv, 65, 67–69, 72, 100n
Aisne River, 30, 51–53, 101n, 103n
Alexander, Gen. Robert, 58, **59**, **60**, 70, 78, 80, 92n, 95n, 99n; background of, 98n; criticism of, 101n
American Expeditionary Forces (AEF), xv–xvi, **12**, 92n, 94n, 95n, 98n, 101, 102n
Ancerviller, 29
Anger, 78
Antozzi, John, 13
Arras, 22
Artillery, xv, xvii, 7, 13, 22, 25, 58, 83, 71, 73, 87–89, 96n, 97n, 98n; eyewitness descriptions of shellings, 24, 94n, 99n, 100n

Audruicq, 21
Autrecourt, 74

Baccarat Sector, 29–32, **33**, 95n
Bar, 73, 75
Battle Monuments Commission, 91n, 96n, 99n, 100n, 101n
"Battle of Watten," 25
bayonets, 33, 99n, 103n
Bazoches, xiv–xv, 47–38, 51, 58, 76–77, 83, 96n4, 97n; Patterson's near death experience at, 40–44, 95n2
B Company, 29, 49, 65, 100n
Bell, Gen. J. Franklin, 12; background of, 93n
Benjamin, Lt. Col. Julian, 14
Bennett, Capt., 30, 35, 75, 80
Berlin, Irving, 93n
Blazer, Lt. Richard R., 30, 38, 51, 55, 69, 72, 78
Blainville, 33
"Blighty," 22, 94n
Boche, 36, 92n, 96n
Boisleux, 22
Bois de Franclieu, 102n
Bois de la Naza, 60
Boissy le Chatel, 35
Bonningues, 21–22, 25–26
Boyelles, 23
Breitwieser, Sgt. Henry J., xvii, 31, 38, 40, 67
British "Tommies," 18, 94n
British Lee Enfield rifles, 21, 81
Brouville, 29, 32
Browning automatic rifle, **81**
Bulger, Maj. Bozeman, 14
Bull, Capt. Charles M., Jr., 36, 48, 58, 69, 72, 75, 78; described by Patterson, 30
Butler, John C., 13

Buzancy, 73
Byrne, Lt. Joseph F., 45, 85; Patterson's report on Byrne's gravesite, 96n

Cackley, Lt., 78
Calais, 18, 21, 27
Camp Upton, 9, 11–15, 17, 80, 93n
Canadian Corps, 25
Carney, Cpl. Frank, 55
Carroll, Cpl. Patrick J., 15, 31, 37, 76; heroic efforts to rescue Patterson at Bazoches, 40–44, 88; Patterson's postwar praise of, 102n, 103n.
Cassidy, Sgt. James A., 31
C Company, 26, 49, 51
Champigneulles, 68, 71
Charlevaux, 63
Charmes, 29
Chateau-Thierry, 33, 35
Chauchat machine guns, 39, 68, 82, 101n, 102n
Cher Ami (Carrier pigeon), **63**, 97n
"Chickenshit," 92n
Church, Lt., 63
Cleveland, Jim, 13, 51
Collins, Lt. Loren F., 49, 69
Connolly, Sgt. Michael, 31; Patterson's postwar praise of, 96n
Conscientious objectors, 11; definition under Selective Servoice Act of 1917, 93n.
"Cooties," 89, 101n
Cornay, 68
Coulommiers, 34, 35.
Crandall, Lt. Elverton C., 13, 66
Cravath & Henderson, 5
Czak, Lt. Tony, xvii, 34

Daescher, Robert, 47
Davis, Forrest, 95n
D Company, 65, 66
Depot Brigade, 11, 12, 15
de Rehm, Charles, 55
discipline, 27, 84, 92n3; Patterson's belief in, 5
Distinguished Service Cross, xiv–xv, **xvii**, 44, 44, 87–89, 93n, 96n, 101n

Donnelly, Cpl. Charles, 76
Dos Passos, John, xix
Doughboys, xiv–xvii, xix, 91n, 92n, 93n, 94n2, 95n3, 97n2, 100n, 101n3, 103n
Dover, 18
Doullens, 22
Drabkin, Jacob, xvii, 66, 100n; Patterson's postwar friendship with, 103n
Duffy, Pvt. Edwin ("Big Ed"), xv, 48; miraculous survival as POW, 76–77
Duffy, Cpl. John, 37, 43, 55, 89, 96n
Duffy, Jim, 13
Dunne, Father Thomas J., **xvii**, 14; wins Distinguished Service Cross, 93n

E Company, 17, 30, 35, 39, 44, 46, 51, 66, 75, 100n; 80th Division, 71
Eiler, Keith, xix
Ellsworth, Capt. Bradford, 13, 51

Fantin, Sgt. Hugo, 67
Faucher, Sgt. Joseph A., 31, 55, 65
F Company, xiv–xvi, xix, 26, 29–30, 42, 51, 55; 63, 65, 69–70, 72, 75, 85; first days of the Meuse-Argonne Battle, 58–59; in Baccarat Sector, 32–34; in Vesle Sector, 36, 45, 47–48
Fere-en-Tardenais, 33, 35, 45, 95n
Fiero, Giuseppi, 47
Finnegan, John P., quoted, 93n
Finucane, Sgt. Peter, xvii, 80, 96n; wins Distinguished Service Cross, 43–44, 88.
Fitzgerald, F. Scott, quoted, 101n
Flames, 33, 65
Fléville, 67, 68, 75, 100n
Fogarty, Joe, 8, 9
Foy, Cpl. Richard, 96n; wins Distinguished Service Cross, 43–44, 89
Folkestone, 18
Forest of Nesle, 35, 36
French soldiers, 32, 35–36, 38–40, 45, 51, 53, 55, 75, 91n, 96n

funk-holes, xvi, 47, 58, 61, 74
Fussell, Paul, quoted, 92n

Gas attacks, xvi, 21, 31, 38, 43, 44, 47, 58, 65, 81, 84, 85, 95n, 98n; effects of described, 96n; Patterson gassed 45, 46
Gaston, Capt. George F., 17
G Company, 29, 30, 46–49, 51, 58, 66, 68–69, 72, 76, 78–79, 83, 100n, 101n
Gennes, 78, 80
Gibson, Lt. Charles DeWolf, **46**
Gillem Board, xv
Givry, 54
Goodwin, Capt., 8, 9
Governors Island, 7
Grandpré, 65, 101n
Graves, Robert, 94n
Gregory, Lt. Gordon, 46, 58, 88
grenades, 32, 43, 58, 61, 72, 82–84
Grez-en-Bourre, 78

Haig, Field Marshal Douglas, 21, 99n
Harkins, Lt. Matthew, 66
Harricourt, 72
Harris, Maj. Duncan, 58
Harvard, Lionel, 25, 44n
Halter, Pvt., 32, 46, 55
Hayes, Lt. Mike, xv, xvii, 32, 36, 51, 58, 59, 81, 63; character of, 30–31; killed at St. Juvin, 65–66, 87–88, 100n; participates in battle near Bazoches, 38–45; wins Distinguished Service Cross, 87–88.
H Company, 30, 34, 46, 51, 58, 61, 68–69
Headquarters Company, 13, 15, 17, 22, 25, 29, 31, 60, 66, 74, 76
Hemingway, Ernest, xix
Henry, Lt. James, 68, 101n
Hillen, Cpl., 38
Hoover, Herbert, xiv
Hyde, Seymour, 13

Italian soldiers, 53, 75, 97n

Johnson, Sgt. Charles F., xv, 31, 38, 50, 67, 71, 85
Johnstone, Capt. Charles E., 29, 46, 69
Jones, Sgt. George F., 31

Karoa, 17, 93n
K Company, 45
Keene, Jennifer, quoted, 102n
Kenyon, Lt. Theodore, 49

L Company, 34, 68
La Besogne, 65
La Cendrière, 51
La Chalade, **46**, 54, 55
La Fleur, Pvt. George, 44, 45
La Florent, 58
Laon, 76
Laino, Cpl. Thomas, 47, 55
Lake Champlain, 8
Lanfear, Pvt. Matthew, 66
la Noue le Coq, 65
Lapham, Capt. Roger, 45, 98n
Leahy, Capt. William D., quoted, 93n
Le Besace, 74, 102n
Le Four de Paris, 58
Lehmkuhl, Capt. Henry M., xvii, 65, 66, 72
Lengel, Edward, quoted, 99n, 102n
Lenihan, Gen. Michael J., 69
Les Islettes, 54, 75
Lewis, Cpl. Albert, 49, 76, 77; Patterson's report to Veterans Bureau regarding wounds to, 103n
Liggett, Gen. Hunter, quoted, 97n, 98n, 99n
Liverpool, 18
Lloyd George, David, quoted, 83n
Lo Bono, Sgt. Joseph, xvii, 31, 37, 55
"Lost Battalion," 49, **63**, **69**, 97n, 103n
"Lost Generation," xvi
Loupeigne, 35
Lowenthal, Pvt. David, 32

Madero, Texas, **6**
Madden, Joe, 31
Madden, Pvt. George, 45

Marcq, 64, 66, 71
Marshall, Gen. George C., xiii; quoted, xiv
Marne River, 32, 34–35
Maverick, Rep. Maury, quoted, 99n
McAllen, Texas, 5, **6**, 7
McCarthy, Lt. Ralph, 30
McCaskey, Lt. Col. Garrison, 14
M Company, 30
Mercury, Sgt. Joseph, 15
Mexican Border, xiv, 5–6
Meuse-Argonne Battle, xv, 55–75, 91n, 98n, 101n; casualties in, xvi, 103n
Middleton, Willoughby, 75, 102n
Mikowski, Stephen, 39
Miller, Cpl. John, xv, 67
minnenwerfers ("minnies'), 24, 39
Montgomery, Virginia, 96n
Montigny, 29, 32
Mont Notre Dame, 35–38, 40, 45–46, 76
Mooso, Pvt. Henry, 96n
Morris, Lt., 78
Mount Vernon, 80
Murphy, Cpl. Thomas, xv, 31, 60
Murphy, Cpl. William, 55

National Guard, xiv, 33, 59, 81, 92n; photographs of Patterson in, **6**, 7
National Security Act of 1947, xv
New York National Guard, xiv, 5, **6**, 7
Nichols, Cpl. Clayton, 58
No Man's Land, 29, 42, 98n

O'Brien, Lt. Charles ("Pat"), 26, 51
O'Donnell, Cpl. James, 66
O'Neale, Lt. Daniel, 49
Ourcq River, 33, 49

Patterson, Cpl. Cyrus, 61
Patterson, Sgt. Dan, 81
Patterson, Margaret, 103n
Patterson, Robert P., xiv–xvii, xix, 12; at Camp Upton, 11–14, 80; at Mexican Border, 5–6; at Plattsburg, 6–9; gassed, 44–45; "greatest adventure" near Bazoches (August 14, 1918), 40–44; in Baccarat sector, 29–34; in England, 18; in Aisne sector, 51–55; on Atlantic Ocean, 17–18; on the Vesle sector, 35–49; participates in Meuse-Argonne Battle, 55–74; photographs of, **xiii**, **xvii**, **xviii**, **6**, 7, **8**, **46**; post-Armistice activities in France, 75–80; postwar relations with men of Company F, 96n; postwar report on the Battle for St. Juvin, 99n; quoted on Jacob Drabkin, 100n; quoted on Patrick Carroll, 102n; quoted on Samuel Silverstein, 103n; quoted on William Ruppertsburg; wins Distinguished Service Cross, 87; with British in Flanders, 21–27.
"PBIs" (Poor Bloody Infantry), 22
Pershing, Gen. John J., **79**, 91n, 96n, 99n2, 101n, 102n
Peterson, Sgt. Frederick W., 31, 58, 68
Pierson, Sgt. Reuben, 58
Plattsburg Officers Training Camps, xiv, xvi, 6, 7, **8**, 9, 12, 13, 15, 93n
Power, Maj. E. Ormonde, 12, 14

Rambervillers, 29
Raucourt, 74
Red Cross, 77, 98n
Reherry, 32
Reid, Lt. Duff, 78, 79
Rheims, 35
Riordan, Lt. John J., 30
River, Anthony, 13
Roosevelt, Franklin D., xiv
Roosevelt, Quentin, 95n
Roosevelt, Theodore, 95n; quoted, xvi
Root, Clark, Buckner & Howland, xiv
Ruelle family, 76
Ruillé Froids Fonds, 78
Ruille, Compte Jean de, 80
Ruppertsburg, Cpl. William ("Ruppie"), 77; Patterson's postwar praise of, 103n
Russell, Cecil, 47
Rygg, Mike, 68

Salvini, Armando, 31, 77
Scott, Cpl. Joseph, 55
Searles, Wallace, 46, 85
Sedan, 74, 75
Selective Service Act of 1917, 93n
Sergy, 33
Seventy-seventh Division, xv, **xvii**, 11, 15, 33, 55, **59**, **64**, 93n2, 94n, 95n2, 96n2, 97n, 99n3, 102n3; marching song of, xvi
Sexfontaines, 76–78
Shedlin, Sgt. Philip, 67
Silverstein, Samuel, xvii, 77; Patterson's postwar friendship with, 96n
Slotkin, Richard, quoted, 103n
Slover, Sgt. William T., 31
Smedberg, Col. William B., 69
Smith, Sgt. Morrell, 22
Soissons, 35
Songs, xvi, 69, 70, 93n, 101n
Souvenirs, 97n, 101n
"Spirit of the Argonne," 57
Springfield rifle, 81–82
Stewart, Sgt. William R., 31
"Stragglers," 63, 99n
Straub, Cpl. Robert A., wins Distinguished Service Cross, 40–44, 88–89
Stimson, Henry L., xiv, xv
St. Juvin, 14, 30, 58, 71–72, 99n, 100n2, 101n2; battle for, 65–68; death of Mike Hayes at, xv, 66, 87–88, 100n
St. Omer, 22, 29
St. Pierremont, 73–75
St. Thibault, **47**, 51
Stokes, Lt. Horace, 49
Stokes mortar, 13, 25, 29
Sweeney, Lt. John L., 66

Taylor, Sgt. Frank, 31
Tepper, Pvt. Meyer, plays prank on Patterson, 70
Thacher, Maj. Archibald, xvi, 12, 35–36, 44, 65, 80, 95n; attack on St. Juvin, 68–69, 100n, 101n; described by Patterson, 14, 30; wins Distinguished Service Cross, 101n

Thirty-seventh Division, 33
Toomey, Edward, 39
Trout, Steven, quoted, xix
Truman, Harry S., xiv, xv
Twenty-eighth Division

Ulness, Pvt. Arthur T., 66, 85, 101n
Ulness, Pvt. Oscar E., 66, 85, 101n

Van Patten, Archie, 45, 85
Varennes, 69, **70**, **72**
Vauxcéré, 51, 53
Verpel, 72
Vesle River, xiv–xv, xvii, 30, 33, 35–49, 51–53, 55, 76, 82, 95n3, 96n, 97n2, 101n, 103n; Patterson's skirmish with Germans along the Vesle, 40–44.
Veterans Bureau, 96n, 100n, 103n
Vidmer, Col. George, xvi, 14, 80, 93n, 96n
Von Ludendorff, Gen. Erich, quoted 102n

War Department, xiv, 15, 100n
Washington, Andrew, 58
Watten, 25, 26, 95n
Weaver, Maj. S. Fullerton, 14, 65
Weinberg, Bugler Marcy, 76
West, Sgt. George, 76
Whittlesey, Capt. Charles, **48**, 49, **63**, **64**, 97n
Williams, Cpl. Franklin, 76
Wittenmyer, Gen. Edmund, 58, 59
Wogatzke, Pvt. Charles W., 39, 85, 95n
World War II, xiii, xiv, xix, 94n, 95n

YMCA, xvii, 101n

Zimmerman, Sgt. Joseph E., 31, 55

www.ingramcontent.com/pod-product-compliance
Lightning Source LLC
Chambersburg PA
CBHW030527080526
44586CB00011B/351